30 Nov 1932

...New England Conservatory

John Williams

...stakovich 4th

...all for this   deeply honored and grateful,

                        Rudolf Serkin.

...and exhausting   Isaac Stern

...est – and that

...remember you by

...Rattle

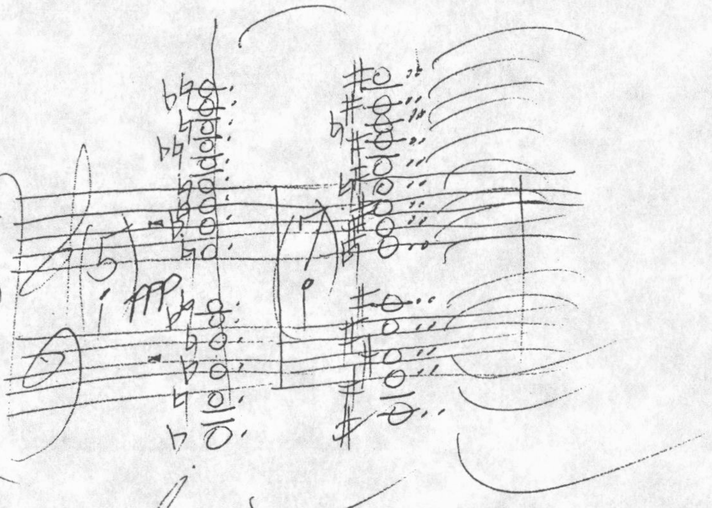

George Crumb

Gustav Holst

April 1929

I am deeply touched and
honored. Thank you with all
my heart.   Josef Gingold

with my great hope that one
day I schall conduct a beautifull
american orchestra, only with american
musicians !

        Dimitri Mitropoulos
            25. 1. 1936

Measure by Measure

Measure by Measure

A History of
New England Conservatory
from 1867

Bruce McPherson

James Klein

Frontispiece: The Conservatory's Beethoven Statue, a favorite place for students to leave notes. The statue, designed by Thomas Crawford, who created the Indian in the Capitol Dome, was originally owned by the Handel and Haydn Society. They loaned it to NEC in 1902, then made it a permanent gift in 1951.

©1995 The Trustees of New England Conservatory of Music

ISBN: 0-9648857-0-0

Credits

Edited by Kelly Stimmell
Design by Shepard Quraeshi Associates
Indexing by Diane Benison
Photo research by Picture Research Consultants and Jean Morrow, Director of New England Conservatory Libraries
Paper by Mohawk Paper Mills
Printed by The Stinehour Press

Photo Credits
Archive Photos, 20, 43 (Paderewski)
The Bettman Archive, 13 (Howe), 26, 51, 98, 108 (jazz band), 119
Boston Athenaeum, 81
Boston Public Library, 82, 85, 92, 96, 105, 106, 107
Boston Symphony Orchestra, 28, 71 (Symphony Hall), 84, 87
The Bostonian Society, 22-23
Isabella Stewart Gardner Museum, 13 (Gardner)
North Wind Picture Archives, 34
Oberlin College Archives, 118
Society for the Preservation of New England Antiquities, 80
Special Collections in Music, University of Maryland, 30
Wide World Photos, 33
All other photographs are from the New England Conservatory Archives.

The Authors
Bruce McPherson, chairman of the Liberal Arts Department at New England Conservatory, has three books and innumerable articles to his name, including *Between Two Worlds: Victorian Ambivalence About Progress, An Education of Value,* and *Nothing But the Best.* He has guided the Conservatory in developing a unique liberal arts faculty and curriculum focusing on the aesthetic, political, economic, and social issues through history that have surrounded the making of music and the lives of musicians. James Klein, a member of the Liberal Arts faculty, is a historian who is now working on a book on Victorian politics.

Acknowledgments

Many people have helped in the writing of this history. It was Laurence Lesser's idea and without his commitment to the project at all points along the way, there would be no book. Nancy Perkins simply made it possible. To both of them we owe a great deal and so too, we believe, does the Conservatory. Gordon Talley patiently, yet finally, marshaled many voices into one coherent manuscript of text, photographs, and design. Kelly Stimmell skillfully copy-edited, mediated, and labored long and hard to complete the myriad details of a book. For that, many thanks. Also, many thanks to Samina Quraeshi and her associates, particularly Marcia Lausen, for their design and creativity; she turned a "pig's tail into a whistle." Jean Morrow provided helpful access to the relevant library resources and also provided elusive facts and information, particularly at the end. Rachel Braude helped with research during the early stages of the work and Claudia Crouse during the latter. Members of the Alumni Affairs Office answered weird questions. Chester Williams, Hankus Netsky, Bob Sullivan, Ran Blake, Andy Falender, Laurence Lesser, Peter Row, and many others provided useful information during the summer of 1992, as we were writing the first draft. Peter Davison made fortuitous comments on the manuscript that hastened its publication. We thank everyone for their help. We are, of course, responsible for what we have written.

New England Conservatory

of Music

Boston, Mass.

Contents

8   Prelude

13   Overture

17   Chapter 1
     Eben Tourjée:
     A Plea for Music

33   Chapter 2
     Eben Tourjée:
     The Largest Conservatory in the World

49   Chapter 3
     Carl Faelton:
     European Customs

55   Chapter 4
     George Whitefield Chadwick:
     Unanimous Choice

63   Chapter 5
     Eben Jordan, 2nd:
     Partner in a Modern Conservatory

83   Chapter 6
     George Whitefield Chadwick:
     An American School

93   Chapter 7
     John Wallace Goodrich:
     The Depression Years

113 Chapter 8
     Harrison Keller:
     Good Times and Bad

131 Chapter 9
     Gunther Schuller:
     The Complete Musician

144 Coda

148 Appendix

151 Index

Prelude

When New England Conservatory was approaching its 125th anniversary, I thought we should seize the opportunity such an occasion affords to explain our passage through those years. Much of our history is palpable: I walk past the statue of our founder, Eben Tourjée, every day. Students still leave notes on the statue of Beethoven, as they have for decades. Performers add to the silent echoes of the past in Jordan Hall at New England Conservatory. The George Whitefield Chadwick Medal is awarded to an outstanding undergraduate every year and, more recently, the Gunther Schuller Medal, to an outstanding graduate student. There is a Brown Hall, a Spaulding Library and a Firestone Library, a Keller Room and a Williams Hall—all named for people who in their different ways built and developed this Conservatory.

But beyond the immediate and everyday reminders of the past, too much of our story had been lost. I asked two members of our faculty to remedy that loss so that as we passed our 125th year, we would know how far we had come. During the summer of 1992, they pieced together the history of this institution from patchy documents and incomplete records. In a locked room in the basement of Jordan Hall at New England Conservatory, they found Tourjée's ledgers of the first years of the Conservatory with the names of the original students and his careful records of the fees they paid. They found letters by Chadwick, partial collections of old catalogs, and alumni bulletins. They visited the old Music Hall and Franklin Square, the Conservatory's two sites before Jordan Hall at NEC was built.

It was clear that, for most of its existence, the Conservatory had focused on the present and the future, and many times had wanted to forget the past (for good reason). But now is a good time to look back and reflect before we gather ourselves and push toward the millennium and then our 150th year. Each year we get better; each year we get stronger. By reading this story, we can see ourselves as part of a long and successful enterprise.

And what a story! We've moved from Tremont Street to Franklin Square to Huntington Avenue. We've had great leaders: Eben Tourjée, George Whitefield Chadwick, and Gunther Schuller. Great faculty: John O'Neill, Carl Faelten, Frederick Converse, Ferruccio Busoni, Antoinette Szumowska, among the early ones, and not-so-long-ago giants such as Gladys Miller, Boris Goldovsky, Richard Burgin, and Lorna Cooke deVaron. Great benefactors:

Tourjée's ledgers

Eben Jordan, 2nd, and George W. Brown. And great students: Nordica, Jesús Sanromá, Eleanor Steber, McHenry Boatwright, and too many in the last quarter century to list by name. Amid the stars and the famous has been a continuous music making by individuals whose small victories have accumulated, echoes caught in the rafters of time, to make an institution where people have lived out their hopes and dreams, where generations have trod. Cumulatively, the Conservatory has added to the store of musical and cultural richness in Boston, America, and the world.

But it wasn't easy. Omnipresent in this story is the stalking presence of failure. Time and again, the Conservatory faced its demise; each time, it slipped by. We've survived depressions, wars, mortgages, recurrent deficits, crashed stock markets, and weak leaders. That there is a Conservatory here now is the result of some incredibly hard work by past trustees, administrators, faculty, and students — and a good shot of luck.

So we celebrate our history as we re-open Jordan Hall at NEC, restored and ready for the future. New England Conservatory has had many men and women who have brought it this far, who have shaped it, nurtured it, loved it, who have passed it on to us as we, in turn, must pass it on as well.

The great Victorian critic, John Ruskin, speaking of the visual arts, once wrote: "Fine art is that in which the hand, the head, and the heart of man go together." He might well have been thinking of music. I know no better description of what happens at New England Conservatory when it is at its best. Those who work and learn here, while confronting the immediacy of the everyday tasks of learning and teaching, also have their gaze set high. This is an institution dedicated to the very best in the musical arts and to the preparation of the next generation to take their place as the shapers and interpreters of our musical culture. For more than 125 years, New England Conservatory has done that. Legions of students, performers, and teachers—famous and anonymous, remembered and forgotten—have added to the earth's store of music, enjoyment, and meaning. This book chronicles some of the dimensions of our story and shows why we can be proud of our institution.

Laurence Lesser
President

Next page: Jordan Hall at NEC in 1990
Below: The Conservatory's first location
on Tremont Street (top) and its current site on
Huntington Avenue (bottom)

OCTOBER 20, 1903

Overture

Out into the gleaming wood, rich bronze decorations, and gilded Corinthian columns boomed Bach's *Toccata and Fugue in C Major* as Wallace Goodrich, one of America's foremost organists, began the inauguration of Jordan Hall at New England Conservatory. Earlier that evening, Boston society, swathed in jewels and furs, had paraded up the steps into the hall. Arriving in horse-drawn carriages, hansom cabs, and on Huntington Avenue's horse-drawn trolley, Boston's music lovers swirled down Huntington Avenue, swelling an impatient crush on Gainsborough Street. Cool autumn air favored the ladies, who had dressed extravagantly. Mrs. Eben Jordan, wife of the hall's benefactor, wore black point d'esprit

over white silk, set off by diamonds. For the short ride from Fenway Court, Isabella Stewart Gardner wore her customary black gown, embellished with a single diamond. Julia Ward Howe, Conservatory trustee and author of "The Battle Hymn of the Republic," dressed in simple white. And Antoinette Szumowska, the evening's piano soloist, wore black chiffon over black silk, with a corsage of violets.

Boston's elite led the "magnificent gathering" of eleven hundred music lovers into Jordan Hall at NEC. They came to show their approval of New England Conservatory, their enthusiasm for the Boston Symphony Orchestra, and their curiosity about the new hall. As they swept in, they found a hall that the *Boston Globe* considered "unequalled the world over." Even the BSO's European musicians, whose old-world sophistication gave them the final word, pronounced it a beautiful place, with unsurpassed acoustics.

After Goodrich concluded, the Boston Symphony took the new stage. Its founder and benefactor, Major Henry L. Higginson, also a Conservatory trustee, entered to thunderous applause. He welcomed the Conservatory to its new location and Jordan Hall at NEC to Boston's musical life. As the man who had brought Boston to musical prominence, he sketched out the evolution of American music from the Puritans, with their incessant psalms, to the nascent music societies, through the days of the Harvard Musical Association, the Music Hall, the Music Academies, the Boston Symphony, Symphony Hall, and now New England Conservatory's new building and crown jewel, Jordan Hall at NEC. He paid tribute to the shapers of the story: Lowell Mason, John Dwight, Theodore Thomas, John Knowles Paine, and Eben Tourjée. He praised the men who had financed it: Richard Dana, Arthur Estabrook, and Charles Gardner. He told of the Conservatory's past; praised its current leader, George Chadwick; reminded its students and graduates of their duty to help it along with their music; then urged men of means to support the Conservatory generously. And he gave gracious thanks to Eben Jordan, 2nd, who had paid for the new hall.

Conservatory trustee Julia Ward Howe (right), one of Boston's prominent citizens, attended the hall's opening night, as did Isabella Stewart Gardner (a detail from John Singer Sargent's famous portrait).
Left: Jordan Hall at NEC and Chadwick's manuscript score

Higginson used the occasion to pass the torch to a new generation of benefactors. As an old Bostonian made rich by railroads and oil, he had given generously to Harvard, then launched the Boston Symphony Orchestra. Now he thanked Jordan for taking up his work, providing music for Boston and America. Jordan's gift, Higginson noted, had not only made the Conservatory whole but also realized the city's musical design. Sitting in the hall named for him, Jordan, a private man, was embarrassed yet gratified by Higginson's praise.

George Whitefield Chadwick, a man with another kind of genius, followed Higginson onto the new stage. The first of a generation of American composers to win an international reputation, he lifted his baton, then led the BSO through his own dramatic overture, *Melpomene*. It was, as one observer noted, "the most dignified, possibly the very best" piece of musical Americana. Both Chadwick and his work were received with "tremendous enthusiasm." He then surrendered the baton to the much-admired conductor of the BSO, Wilhelm Gericke, who led his orchestra in Schumann's Concerto in A Minor, before closing the evening with Beethoven's *Eroica*. Even Gericke's notoriously demanding musicians recognized that Jordan Hall at NEC was "altogether magnificent, the most glorious of instrumental sounds that we can recall in America." As one explained, "We never knew the full glory of our orchestra."

JORDAN HALL
New England Conservatory of Music
October 20th, 1903

INAUGURAL CONCERT
BY THE
Boston Symphony Orchestra
Mr. WILHELM GERICKE, Conductor

Mme. ANTOINETTE SZUMOWSKA, Pianist
Mr. WALLACE GOODRICH, Organist

PROGRAM

Prelude }
Fugue } in C major for organ,   Bach

Address,
          Mr. HENRY L. HIGGINSON

Dramatic Overture, " Melpomene,"   Chadwick
             Conducted by the Composer

Concerto in A minor,   Schumann
      Allegro affettuoso — Intermezzo, Andantino grazioso
                  Allegro vivace

Symphony in E-flat (Eroica)   Beethoven
         Allegro con brio — Marcia funebre
         Scherzo — Finale, Allegro molto. Presto

is invited to inspect the Conservatory building at the close of

MASON & HAMLIN PIANOFORTE USED

Renowned BSO conductor Wilhelm Gericke showed off the hall's superb acoustics by conducting his Symphony in Schumann and Beethoven.

Front page of the Globe, *October 21, 1903*

Bostonians who attended that concert—and those who read about it the next day—could be proud of their new hall, for the opening of Jordan Hall at NEC marked the culmination of a long struggle to serve the city and its musical tradition. From the Museum of Fine Arts to Symphony Hall, Huntington Avenue now fulfilled the dreams and entrepreneurial energy of Boston's leading citizens. New England Conservatory radiated "works in progress" from its new center, Jordan Hall at NEC. Here, budding talents were disciplined and initiated into music. Here, culture drew upon the past to educate the present and explore the future.

Boston audiences recognized and appreciated serious music. They listened to America's finest orchestra play demanding works from an international repertoire. They welcomed a new generation of American composers, many of whom, such as Chadwick, Frederick Converse, and Arthur Foote, taught at the Conservatory.

It didn't take long for Boston's crown jewel, Jordan Hall at NEC, to attract the world's finest musicians, among them cellist Pablo Casals.

And they gloried in the debut of Jordan Hall at NEC. The hall quickly became a fixed venue on the concert round, attracting some of the world's preeminent performers, including Ferruccio Busoni, the Italian pianist and composer (who also served on the faculty); Victor Maurel, the great French baritone whom Verdi had chosen to sing Falstaff and Iago; Pablo Casals, the young cellist; and an even younger Arthur Rubinstein. Years later, Rubinstein recalled that Jordan Hall at NEC "felt more like Europe than anywhere else in America."

After the famous artists performed and their audiences dispersed, Jordan Hall at NEC resumed its role as the heart of a great conservatory. Students who ushered at the concerts of the famous returned to their daily discipline of practice, analysis, and more practice. For them, the hall became a meeting ground, rehearsal space, and stage for public performance. Above all, it became a symbol of their aspirations. "I still get a feeling of nervousness when I go to Jordan Hall at NEC," said Harry Ellis Dickson '29. "I remember how excited I was to perform there as a student."

The glory of Jordan Hall at NEC is the story of New England Conservatory. But that story needed more than Eben Jordan's generosity or George Chadwick's genius to reach its great success on that night in October 1903. It needed a man who could dream of such successes where there were only hymns, dance halls, and railroad galops. It needed Eben Tourjée.

15

EBEN TOURJÉE:
A PLEA FOR MUSIC

1

Our leaders all were gallant men—
Eichberg—Gilmore—Tourjée—Zerrahn.
—*Major Alfred Little*, About the Jubilee

In June 1853 a nineteen-year-old music
teacher caught Providence's morning train
to Boston. He arrived in Old Colony Depot,
rode the horse-car downtown, and entered
the new Music Hall, off Tremont Street.
There, in a small office on the second floor,
he met some of the city's musical leaders,
among them John Dwight, editor of the
influential *Dwight's Journal of Music;* Dr. J.
Baxter Upham, president of the Harvard
Musical Association; and Oliver Ditson, the
city's leading publisher of sheet music.
Ditson, who had taken an interest in that
young educator, introduced his colleagues to
Eben Tourjée. Tourjée then explained his
ideas for a conservatory taught through
the "class system," rather than by individual
lessons. Boston, he argued, needed and
wanted such an enterprise. His listeners,
who envied the schools of Leipzig, Paris, and
Munich, recognized Boston's need but were
unsure of this energetic little man and his
unorthodox ideas.

Tourjée explained that his "class
system" of instruction, adapted from
European models, would make a conservatory both popular and economical. He
urged his belief in the power of music and
in the need to train outstanding young
musicians. The Bostonians listened, then
asked the amiable young enthusiast to wait
for their answer.

So an excited Tourjée toured Boston.
He introduced himself to Lowell Mason,
longtime champion of music education in
public schools, and told him of his plans
for a conservatory. That night, he stayed at
the YMCA. The next day he called on Ditson
to hear the verdict: the group had rejected
his plan. It was, they said, not the time
to risk such a venture, nor did they see any
hope of attracting enough students to make
it work. National affairs were uncertain.
The country was already embroiled in the
recurrent crises that would culminate in the
Civil War. Besides political and economic
uncertainty, though, the musical leaders had
practical doubts about Tourjée and his
scheme. A self-taught church organist, he
inspired no great confidence in his musicali-
ty. Dwight, who adamantly opposed
Tourjée's ideas, announced that he should
"catch the next train back to Providence."
His first assault on America's musical world
rejected, young Tourjée beat a retreat to
Rhode Island.

*Music Hall, center of Boston's mid-nineteenth-
century musical activity, off Tremont Street*

*Eben Tourjée, founder of New England
Conservatory. He was told, "It would be no
more possible to establish a conservatory in
this country than to make a whistle out of a
pig's tail."*

But he would be back. Thirteen years later, in December 1866, Tourjée again visited the Music Hall and laid his plan before the city's leading musicians. This time Carl Zerrahn, Boston's most prominent conductor, and Charles Perkins, patron of the arts (and later donor of the Beethoven statue outside Jordan Hall at NEC), joined Upham, Ditson, and Dwight at the meeting. Tourjée was accompanied by his Providence colleagues, Franklin Snow and Robert Goldbeck.

This time, the unorthodox educator won over his audience. The times had changed: the end of the Civil War, the rapid growth of the economy, and a heightened interest in music had created a growing need for musicians and musical education. And during the interim, Tourjée had proven himself in Rhode Island, where he had created three music schools. Now, these Bostonians agreed to help him launch his New England Conservatory of Music.

Tourjée knew what was required. First, he had to find a site. So he signed an agreement to rent seven rooms above the Music Hall. Then, he needed faculty. So he hired as many of Boston's musicians as he could find. Finally, he needed students. So he papered the city with fliers, posters, and handbills, advertising talented teachers and cheap lessons. On February 18, 1867, he opened the doors to New England Conservatory.

Despite his hopes, it was not an auspicious beginning, for NEC was not Boston's first music school. Only a week before the Conservatory opened, Julius Eichberg, a well-known violinist, had opened his own Boston Conservatory. Tourjée, who had hoped to use that name himself, had to regretfully opt for New England Conservatory. *Dwight's Journal* observed that two days before the Boston Conservatory opened, Eichberg had already enrolled 130 students when "by a sudden *coup d'état* a New England Conservatory dropped down from the clouds, captured the Music Hall, flooded Boston with grandiloquent Circulars, created 'Professors' by the score, and, gathering up pupils fast, is ready to open...." Despite his difficulties, Tourjée

Dwight's Journal of Music.

WHOLE No. 920.   BOSTON, SATURDAY, JULY 22, 1876.   VOL. XXXVI. No. 8.

John Dwight's lack of confidence in Tourjée's ability to start Boston's first conservatory of music was one of Tourjée's greatest hurdles.

Carl Zerrahn, Boston's most prominent conductor in the mid-nineteenth century, supported Tourjée's mission for a European-modeled conservatory.

Julius Eichberg officially took the name The Boston Conservatory for his school a week before Tourjée was to open the doors of his conservatory under the same name, leaving Tourjée to settle for New England Conservatory.

Journal of Music.

ON, SATURDAY, MAY 15, 1875.   VOL. XXXV. No. 3.

A sample Dwight's Journal of Music, *the musical authority of Boston*

managed to attract 392 students that first month. By September he had enrolled 620; by December, 744. Even though most of his students were only part-time, Tourjée's Conservatory was on its way.

Tourjée quickly moved to consolidate his new institution. In doing so, he gave full scope to his genius, advertising, organizing, and converting everyone who crossed his path. Within a month, he presented NEC's inaugural concert. His "suddenly arrived institution" offered a program that included an original piano concerto by his co-director, Goldbeck; an organ performance by Harvard's Professor of Music John Knowles Paine; and a song by Hattie Sterling, an NEC student from New York. The hodgepodge of serious, popular, and religious music was, as *Dwight's Journal* complained, "rather mixed, and not much after a Leipzig or any classically educated model." But it proclaimed a new voice on the Boston musical scene: an entrepreneurial institution, led by an impresario determined to catch the public ear.

Dwight's Journal had exclaimed that new conservatories were dropping from the sky. But such institutions, particularly New England Conservatory, arose from the conjunction of several forces at work in post-war America. Amid its strenuous prosperity, the country was already calling for "culture," especially for one that was distinctly American. Musicians, once the most mistrusted of the country's artists, now found themselves besieged by a middle class that wanted high culture, great art, and piano lessons. They responded by joining—or inventing—a host of musical institutions: academies, conservatories, and schools

of music. A generation earlier, Lowell Mason had convinced Boston to teach music in the public schools. From that had grown a new generation of promising artists—and increasingly sophisticated audiences—that spread, and deepened, the call for music. Now a new generation of philanthropists, prospering in the heroic days of industrial expansion, helped launch and sustain the schools, halls, and orchestras that serious music required.

Boston, the nation's cultural leader, however, wanted music that was both recognizably great and identifiably American. It was not enough to provide stages, audiences, and incomes for European musicians; the country had to develop its own native talent. Eastern cities housed a prosperous managerial class with money to spend on leisure and culture. Middle-class women, shut out from political and business careers, turned to education and the arts. As a result, the demand for—and taste in—music bloomed.

Harvard's Professor of Music, John Knowles Paine, "known as the dean of American music," performed at the Conservatory's first concert in Music Hall.

Little more than a decade earlier, in 1852, *Dwight's Journal* had lamented the "confused, crude, heterogeneous sudden musical activity in a young utilitarian people." The record of performances bore out that criticism. Music in antebellum America offered a mixture of simple piety and crass commercialism that appalled sophisticates like Dwight, Ditson, and Upham. Audiences flocked to hear celebrities, rather than talents: P.T. Barnum's incessant advertising for Swedish soprano Jenny Lind had won over reluctant ticket-buyers and set the model for "serious" music. American audiences craved amusement and cared little for the niceties of composition. They fled in terror from Brahms, tolerated Beethoven, and cheered the *Railroad Galop* to the echo. That monotonous melody, a variation on thousands like it, consisted of an entire orchestra tooting accompaniment while a model train, set on elaborate tracks, circled the stage. Between 1850 and 1870, it was the most popular piece in American concerts. Musicians, conductors, and cultural leaders such as Dwight loathed it, but people paid money to see and hear that train.

Lowell Mason was the first to champion music courses in the public school curriculum, a cause Tourjée eventually took on when he founded the National Music Congress.

Long before Tourjée, Lowell Mason, Dwight's longtime friend, was one of the first musical pioneers to try to change America's taste for hymns and whistles. His Academy of Music, launched in 1833, had educated large numbers of students. In 1837 he had convinced Boston to include music courses in the public school curriculum—the first such classes in America. His success spawned imitations in New York, Philadelphia, and Providence, while a new generation of educators—including Tourjée—extended his work. Tourjée founded a Fall River Musical Institute in 1853, a Newport Musical Institute in 1858, and a School of Music at the East Greenwich Academy in 1859. In 1864 he created the Providence Institute of Music. Chartered in 1865 as the Providence Conservatory of Music, it became America's first conservatory. Such conservatories soon sprang up across America: Oberlin Conservatory opened its doors in 1865, Baltimore's Peabody Institute appeared in 1868, and Cincinnati hired Theodore Thomas, America's most famous conductor, to launch its conservatory in 1878.

Thus, Tourjée was only one of a host of enthusiastic musicians and teachers setting up these academies, conservatories, and musical colleges. What set him apart was the missionary zeal with which he promulgated music. For Tourjée, music was a religious calling, a way of serving God. He insisted that "to deny these young folk the opportunity to encourage this talent is to renounce our obligation to God."

America's new class of capitalists recognized more secular obligations. In a single generation, Boston's philanthropists launched the cultural and educational institutions that helped their city strengthen its heritage as America's cultural leader. In the twenty years after the Civil War, they endowed the Museum of Fine Arts, Boston University, and the Boston Symphony Orchestra. A generation later, at the turn of the century, Eben Jordan, 2nd, followed their example, entirely endowing the present Conservatory building.

Money was always Eben Tourjée's great concern. The Music Hall charged him a "reasonable rent," but he relied on tuition fees to pay that rent and salaries. So, the search for students occupied him all the time. For that reason, he joined with Robert Goldbeck, one of New England's best-known pianists and music teachers. They became co-directors of NEC. Goldbeck attracted talented pianists, while Tourjée oversaw the business of soliciting other students and teachers.

The arrangement didn't last. Born in Potsdam, Germany, Goldbeck enjoyed a certain reputation as a performer, and Tourjée needed him to provide the musicianship while he saw to more practical matters. But Goldbeck didn't get on with his fellow teachers, many of whom were Americans with budding reputations of their own. His Prussian manners made him no more popular with his students. More to the point, he and Tourjée squabbled over tuition rates and dubious candidates for admission. Tourjée wanted to undercut the market by offering lessons at the lowest possible cost; that had been the secret of his earlier successes. So he set modest fees: individual lessons for as little as forty cents, 125 hours of class instruction for only fifteen dollars. Nor was he especially fastidious about a prospect's talent. He seemed to find potential in anyone willing to pay for help in developing it. One aspiring pianist recalled that all he had to do to pass his audition was find a C chord. Low tuition and minimal standards attracted a throng of students and made the "class" method profitable. But such tactics did little to further the idea of a conservatory modeled along the lines of European professionalism.

By the spring of 1867, Tourjée and Goldbeck were no longer on speaking terms. That fall, Tourjée pushed his colleague aside and became the Conservatory's sole director. His victory meant the school would be less European than Goldbeck had hoped; Goldbeck's more professional vision had the support of Boston's musical experts, but his later failures in St. Louis and Chicago suggested that America's students were not yet ready for his international style of music education. With the Conservatory, Tourjée, who even his fondest friends conceded was "not a deeply educated musician," operated a freewheeling American business that occasionally offended the sensibilities of his betters but did much to popularize serious music.

Tourjée had other, equally impressive —some might even say better—talents. He showed a deep sympathy for students, whatever their means or abilities. As they later recalled, he haunted the offices and classrooms, accosted students in the halls, preached brief, encouraging sermons, and concentrated his considerable energies on making them feel that they were part of a great idea and a happy home. He focused the same talent and persuasiveness on attracting outstanding teachers, whose skills more than compensated for his own shortcomings. And he threw himself into the evangelical work of converting America to the cause of classical music. An alumnus recalled hearing him in distant California, giving "one of his earnest pleas for music and its elevation in his country." Tourjée talked of neither talent nor business sense, but of dedication: "He sang a simple, unaccompanied song, which brought tears to the eyes…. His religion and his love for the Conservatory went hand in hand, and there was no doubt of the sincerity of either."

His dedication and hard work turned a handful of empty rooms into a conservatory. The materials were hardly promising. One of his first students recalled that "the rooms were bare and unattractive, even to dinginess, seven chairs and a piano constituted the furniture and the evidences of the lack of money were on every side." Tourjée's office was no more than a "cubbyhole…over the stairway" with a small piano and a tiny rolltop desk. Charles Denée, one of the school's early teachers, recalled a private meeting with the director: "We nearly filled the remaining space when the door was closed." In such unpromising facilities, students found Tourjée "rushing about, attempting to do everything himself, and as he often said, he 'had some fish to fry.'" He also had to fry them in two places at the same time. During that first year, he commuted between Boston and Providence, where his family remained and his old conservatory was winding down its affairs. On top of it all, he was struck by personal loss. His wife, Abbie, died suddenly that frantic October. Although he reeled under the blow, he returned to Boston and his Conservatory, accompanied by his mother and three small children.

Less than a year into his new work, he began to consider expansion. As enrollments rose and classes grew crowded, he was forced to borrow more rooms to hold lessons. So in January 1868 he persuaded Upham to rent him additional space in the Music Hall. By December, he had twenty-five classrooms and 1,414 students. Within a decade, his Conservatory had reached its limit, with 2,040 students occupying three floors of the Music Hall annex. By 1885, he had 4,570 students.

Conservatory students held concerts in the Music Hall once every term, four times a year. And they listened as more distinguished performers appeared on the same stage. The Harvard Musical Association, Handel & Haydn Society, and Theodore Thomas and his orchestra all played there. So did some of the great European artists: Hans von Bülow, Wagner's favorite conductor and former husband of the formidable Cosima Wagner herself, and Ignacy Paderewski, whose long hair made his appearance as remarkable as his piano playing. Lillian Norton, who later starred on both American and European stages herself, long remembered the thrill of squeezing through the upper-floor windows of the Music Hall and listening, rapt, while her heroes performed the music she loved.

The interior of the 2,500-seat Music Hall,
home to the Conservatory's first concerts

Ever one for advertising, Tourjée trumpeted those occasions. By November 1873, he calculated that his Conservatory had held 306 of these Music Hall concerts. Even by his standards, that was a brisk pace. Not every one was a success; *Dwight's Journal* occasionally commented on the "untoward accidents" that attended those "quiet little Conservatory concerts." But they were often critically acclaimed; even *Dwight's Journal* conceded that B.J. Lang's debut of Saran's *Fantasie in the Form of a Sonata* was "fresh and full of genius; since the sonatas of Beethoven few better than this." Those concerts emphasized piano, organ, and voice, musical areas that reflected both student interest and ability. The rival Boston Conservatory of Music, on the other hand, featured violins to highlight both the talents of its director and the "shower of youthful violinists" he attracted.

In competition with Eichberg and Boston Conservatory, NEC enjoyed three advantages that were to prove decisive: First, the fast-rising success of NEC alumna Lillian Norton, or "Nordica," as she came to be known. Second, the overwhelming publicity for the Conservatory generated by the Peace Jubilees. And third, the beneficial alliance between NEC and the BSO.

In 1868, Tourjée—or his finest voice teacher, John O'Neill—attracted a young singer from Maine who had almost no training but showed enormous talent and appetite for work. Decades later, Lillian Norton, that promising vocalist, became the reigning diva of her age, although she confessed that her greatest achievement was surviving O'Neill's "four years of fault-finding." Norton described her study with O'Neill at New England Conservatory as "stained with tears and sodden with discouragement." To pay for her lessons, she

worked, went without meals, and withstood years of genteel poverty. She suffered, and O'Neill did nothing to encourage her. He even refused to let her perform, brusquely insisting, "You will sing when I tell you to, but not before." He relented only after two years of study, allowing her to debut with *"Tacea la Notte"* from *Il Trovatore* at a student performance in June 1874. She finished her NEC career by singing Bellini's *"Care Campagne"* from *La Sonnambula* at the 1875 graduation.

Using the stage name Nordica, Lillian Norton was to become the Conservatory's brightest jewel, polished and set by O'Neill. And despite her suffering under his tutelage, she gave full credit to him for the rest of her life. An admirer who heard her sing in Brescia, Italy, told the American press that "Miss Norton gives the credit for her vocal culture solely to Mr. O'Neill of the New England Conservatory of Music, from whom alone she has received vocal lessons." She won international fame, even performing the role of Brunhilde in Bayreuth, Germany. The once impoverished student earned staggering sums: the Chicago Opera paid her $10,000 for a single season, the Boston Opera Company, $2,500 for one performance; a brief tour of the West earned her $40,000. But she never forgot her alma mater, and the Conservatory understandably celebrated her success. Tourjée even staged a "Welcome Return" in 1883 to honor his most distinguished alumna. To show her appreciation, Nordica sang one of Chopin's *Nocturnes*, personally arranged for her by Riccardo Drigo, "Director of the Imperial Opera and sung at his Court by request of the late Czar, Alexander II." Her career was Tourjée's bright, shining star. Her success helped to launch his school.

Name	No.	Address
Anchor Mrs A. J.	10 318 342	26 Chester Park
Back Ida	12	12 E Springfield St
Bruce Florence J	16 348	9 Temple St
Bell Clara	19 163 219	Somerville
Brickes Wm J	20	73 Brookline St
Bramhall Alice	27	9 Warren Place
Briggs Ella	34 43	38 Union Park
Baser Frances A.	39 24 400	46 No Bennet St
Bowes Alice	44 19	16 Church St
Bullard O B.	46	
Brewster Miss E.	53	30 Hancock St
Butler Annie D	59	Waverly Mass
Bacheller Miss L	71	Lynn Mass
Brown Chas E.	90	42 Concord Sq
Baser Miss M.	95	Warren St Roxbury
Bruce Fannie	134 24	Centre St Cambridgeport
Blackmore John W		So Boston
Barnard Mrs A. W.		Lynn
Bonney Avonia		dgeport
Bean Wm M M		Chelsea
Barnard S. R		Lynn
Baser Louise		So Boston
Belcher Mrs A. A		
Burrett Adele		
Beechey Mary		
Barrows Wm E J		
Bailey Wm A. S.		Roxbury
Bamford Mr A		Roxbury
Bunday Wm H S		
Bailey Wm J S		Cambridgeport
Bemis Miss E		
Bemis May		
Bacheller Annie		
Bosson H F.		Chelsea
Brown Miss M.	319 19	48 Charter St
Bright Wm H V.	321	Broadway Cambridgeport
Bartlett Mrs M. E	322	Lynn Mass
Brett Mr A E.	336	18 Broadway St

That same year, Tourjée had seized on an even more spectacular opportunity to promote the Conservatory and to popularize musical events. He buttonholed Patrick Gilmore, a self-made patriot who came to America via the large wave of Irish immigration. During the Civil War, Gilmore had created his own brass band, then served with it in the 24th Massachusetts Volunteers. Like Tourjée, he was a musical democrat, eager to popularize music. His own work included "When Johnny Comes Marching Home," a tune that, he insisted, an angel had given him.

In 1868 the angel reappeared, commanding him to produce an extravaganza for music and for America: a Peace Jubilee. So Gilmore mobilized a choir of ten thousand, an orchestra of a thousand—complete with one hundred cannons and a twenty-five-foot drum—and one hundred Boston firemen to hammer out Verdi's *Anvil Chorus.* To house them, he envisioned a coliseum seating fifty thousand. To pay for it all, he needed financial assistance, as much as $200,000. Politicians and philanthropists in New York and Washington refused, but Boston's Eben Jordan, Sr., agreed to help, provided "you can get Professor Tourjée as choral director." Gilmore quickly enlisted his new ally. When Jordan agreed to serve as the Jubilee's treasurer, "fourteen thousand dollars were raised in as many minutes."

All that remained was to build an auditorium, find more than a thousand instrumentalists, search out ten thousand singers, and raise the rest of the money—in four months. Gilmore began by setting up his command post at NEC. From there, Tourjée sent directives across America, appealing for help. He also offered advice on forming choral societies where none existed, even handing out free music books.

He sent assistants to help fledgling groups, provided programs, and proselytized whole communities. With an eye fixed on the future, he campaigned for "the awakening of the greater interest in the art, and the attainment of a higher standard of sacred music." His work not only publicized the Conservatory but helped create a new pool of students.

It also aligned the school with Gilmore and the democrats against musical elitists like John Dwight and Carl Zerrahn, for the festival, officially named the "National Peace Jubilee," met with spectacular popular success. On June 15, 1869, vast crowds filled Gilmore's new coliseum (built over the muddy flats that became Copley Square) to watch for "the first time in the history of music, 10,000 singers and 1,000 musicians brought together under one baton." The performance began with "A Mighty Fortress Is Our God," followed by "See, the Conquering Hero Comes"—

Gilmore's tribute to his most distinguished guest, President Ulysses S. Grant. His gargantuan orchestra then performed popular and patriotic airs, including the overture from *Tannhäuser*, excerpts from Rossini's *Stabat Mater*, and snippets from instrumental and choral pieces by Bach, Mozart, Schubert, Haydn, Handel, Mendelssohn, Beethoven, and Meyerbeer. Gilmore, Zerrahn, Eichberg, and Tourjée conducted in shifts, trying to impose order on ensembles that had come from all across America and Europe, had never rehearsed together, and could barely hear themselves over the din. Gilmore opted for effect, rather than quality: he set Madame Parepa-Rosa to sing *Ave Maria* in front of two hundred violins. President Grant enjoyed the ensuing sparks of the hundred red-shirted firemen beating time to Verdi's *Anvil Chorus* so much that Gilmore repeated the spectacle for him.

Purists detested those shenanigans. *Dwight's Journal* insisted that America's concertgoers cared "more for…unquestioned masterworks than for any novelty, more for the music than for the performer, more for the matter than the manner, more for Art than for the personality of any artist." When the Jubilee revealed a less cultured, more populist approach, it denounced Gilmore for catering to "the caprices of fashion and the tricks of advertisement." Dwight himself had fled Boston, rather than listen to all those voices, violins, and anvils. But there was no arguing with the bottom line: Gilmore not only turned a profit estimated at $50,000 but roused the musical curiosity of the world. Choruses from Ohio, violinists from Missouri, and brass bands from Europe descended on Copley Square to prove Gilmore's angel a prophet: there was not only an audience for music but an enthusiasm for performing, so much so that Tourjée and Gilmore organized another, even larger, jubilee in 1872, the "World Peace Jubilee."

Thousands of music lovers flocked to the Natinal Peace Jubilee to hear 10,000 singers and 1,000 musicians with 100 cannons and a 25-foot drum perform in Verdi's Anvil Chorus.

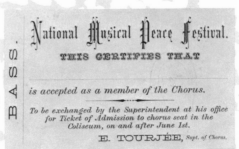

The peace jubilees attracted musicians from all corners of the United States and the globe.

The elitists were slow to respond to Gilmore's spectacle. But when they did, they offered an alternative vision of music that was less noisy, but no less impressive. In the spring of 1881, Major Henry Higginson published his famous letter, "In Re the Boston Symphony Orchestra," in which, to the cheers of Dwight and his circle, he promised to fund an independent orchestra that was to play a regular program of "serious concerts" and "in the summer, concerts of a lighter kind of music." He would hire musicians, rent halls, and underwrite performances. His musicians were to play exclusively for his BSO, but they might also teach at New England Conservatory. Despite that great fillip, Higginson did not fully endorse Tourjée or his school; he concluded with a cry for "a good, honest school for musicians. Of course it would

Founder of the BSO, Major Henry Lee Higginson encouraged the alliance between the Symphony and NEC.

The Boston Symphony Orchestra, circa 1881: since its inception, the Symphony has turned to the Conservatory for musicians. (Note the Beethoven statue in its original home.)

cost us money, which would be well spent." Higginson had attended the Leipzig and Munich conservatories; he still had serious doubts about the church organist and his unorthodox methods.

Nevertheless, nineteen of Higginson's musicians began to teach at NEC in 1881. For more than a century, the careers of his orchestra and the Conservatory were to be intertwined. For the orchestra, NEC provided additional work, opportunities to explore new music, and the gratification of educating a new generation of performers. For the Conservatory, the BSO offered outstanding teachers, a demanding repertoire, and the prestige of intimacy with one of America's finest symphonic orchestra. The two were to grow together, even as they served separate missions.

Higginson's orchestra gave Tourjée a model of professionalism, an institution to which his graduates might aspire, and a quality of performance that made Boston the center of American music. More than that, the Boston Symphony acted as a powerful magnet, pulling NEC away from Gilmore's musical opportunism, toward Higginson's vision of genius and Dwight's hope for a classical conservatory.

Within the walls of the Music Hall, Tourjée and his colleagues began to brood over the need for expansion. Their first class, twelve women and one man, graduated in June 1870. Tourjée exhorted them to persevere, for "in music, as in religion, only those who bear its crosses are permitted to wear its crown." Over the next decade he began to forge the future of the Conservatory and its curriculum in a jumble of both farsighted and opportunistic moves—the essential tension that drove him and gave shape to his Conservatory. He linked his school to the newly founded Boston University in 1872— a brief and unfruitful liaison. He sent Luther Mason off to teach his class method in Japan—an international effort that was richly rewarded in the next century, when Japanese students, trained in "Mason-song," returned to the Conservatory in large and growing numbers.

As director of America's largest conservatory, Tourjée convened the National Music Congress (NMC) in 1869, the first national assembly of music teachers and the foundation of a national commitment to the teaching of music. From the NMC's annual meetings grew the National Music Teachers' Association, organized in 1876 by Theodore Presser, one of the "Doctor's Boys" (a pet nickname used for Tourjée's most talented male graduates), and founder of the music magazine, *Étude*. Tourjée also found time to serve as the association's first president. In 1874 he helped form the Normal Musical Institute "to train and qualify teachers for music instruction in the public schools." This program, taught in the summer by his Conservatory faculty, gave students an opportunity to continue and extend their musical training. It attracted some four hundred people a year, many of them senior students or graduates of the Conservatory.

Such initiatives bubbled out of Tourjée's fertile imagination. In 1878 he launched a series of summer trans-Atlantic trips to Europe, chartered by Thomas Cook and attended by enthusiastic music students from across America. For Tourjée, the voyages combined musical education, European culture, and sight-seeing. His 1881 tour of the Holy Land introduced a fourth crucial interest: his dedication to Christianity. But he had no less interest in fun; his trips were famous for their good humor, antics, and evenings of popular song.

Back in Boston, he threw himself into the public realm. He agreed to help Gilmore concoct a second festival, the World Peace Jubilee, accepted the presidency of the city's YMCA, and organized a settlement house in the slums of Boston's North End.

At the Conservatory, he expanded his curriculum to include painting, drawing, oratory, and elocution, each discipline offered in its own dignified "School" or "College." This proliferation of subjects and departments was a symptom of his restless zeal to enroll ever larger numbers of students, rather than a genuine commitment to "general education" for musicians. His concern for fee-paying students shaped the future of his school: he wanted it to be both a conservatory and a college, a school and an academy. He also wanted it to be a Boston institution, not a handful of rented rooms in the Music Hall.

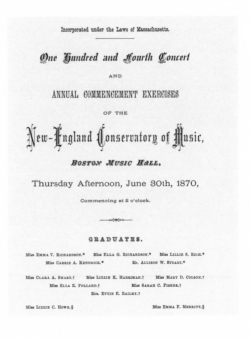

The Conservatory's first commencement exercises in 1870

LUTHER MASON:
THE CONSERVATORY'S
MUSICAL AMBASSADOR
TO JAPAN

By the late 1870s, Eben Tourjée had successfully championed music education in the nation's public schools by helping to establish the National Music Congress and the National Music Teachers' Association. In 1879, the Conservatory's sphere of musical influence stretched beyond the United States to include Japan.

A fluke meeting between Eben Tourjée and the Japanese minister to the United States while they were both vacationing on Block Island led to this, the Conservatory's first international effort. Japan was just beginning to integrate Western music into its own traditional system of music, and the Japanese minister and the National Institute of Music in Toyko wanted an American voice teacher.

Luther Whiting Mason was a natural choice. An esteemed teacher of music for public schools, Mason also taught "Vocal Music in the Public Schools" at the Conservatory and was a part of the New England Normal Institute, a one-month summer pedagogical program held at Tourjée's old alma mater, the East Greenwich Academy, along with Tourjée himself, H. E. Holt, and Alexander Graham

Bell. During his tenure at NEC, Mason also wrote *National Music Course*, the first music textbook for all grades, and was instrumental in developing the Public School Music Department for the National Education Association.

Mason stayed in Japan as governmental supervisor until 1882, and his stay was highly successful. He brought NEC's method of voice instruction to 30,000 Japanese schools. In 1887, the *Musical Herald* reported that Mason's labors in Japan resulted in "a country now in possession of an organized music school, embracing a course extending over four years which includes, in connection with instruction upon Japanese instruments, the same studies which are pursued in our own institutions of that kind. The success and promise of the enterprise are already established."

In appreciation of Mason's efforts, the Japanese government donated native musical instruments to the Conservatory's museum of musical instruments. Today, Japan still remembers both Tourjée and Mason. In 1993, Professor Hiroshi Yasuda wrote a book for Japanese readers on Tourjée. And Mason's teaching system, affectionately dubbed "Mason-Song" by the Japanese, is a term that still lingers in Japan's vocabulary.

TOURJÉE: THE JOHNNY APPLESEED OF MUSIC

Although the artistic value of the peace jubilees of 1869 and 1872 was considered dubious by many of Boston's musical leaders, they did succeed on one important count: to stimulate public interest in music across the nation and throughout the world.

That goal was crucial to the passionate Eben Tourjée, for whom music was a second religion. As choral director, he used the peace jubilees to promote its importance and, in the process, turned into a musical Johnny Appleseed, sowing the seeds for a growth in music across the continent.

First, Tourjée sent his assistants on a mission for the 1869 National Peace Jubilee. They criss-crossed the country, forming choral societies whose members were then encouraged to join the jubilee chorus. "The cause of music demands this action," Tourjée said. "It will be attended with lasting good to the communities and to the entire country." The response was overwhelming: 10,000 trekked to Boston to take part.

After the jubilee ended, Tourjée suggested the various choral groups become permanent. Many did, and love of music started to blossom in towns from East to West.

Tourjée continued to travel the back roads and city highways of America with a slightly different plea: music education in all public schools. In 1869 he spoke before the National Music Congress on developing a uniform system for teaching music in public schools. In 1870 he addressed the National Music Teachers' Association in Cleveland, Ohio, with his speech, "A Plea for Vocal Music in Public Schools," imploring the necessity of music for all classes of people.

"It is the boast of our American school system that all classes, the poor as well as the rich, share its advantages. Hitherto, a musical education, from its high cost, has been confined to the abodes of the wealthy. Shall our poorer citizens, equally susceptible of cultivation, and whose limited means of enjoyment render it a more positive necessity, be debarred its pure and innocent delights?"

The U.S. Office of Education was so inspired by Tourjée's words that it published his speech as a public document, causing many communities to incorporate music into their public school curricula.

Tourjée didn't stop there. He made sure that he passed the torch down to his students, so that they would continue his mission into the next generation. In his 1870 Commencement address to the Conservatory's first graduating class, he said, "Some of you will doubtless now exchange the position of pupil for that of teacher. You will go out to labor as missionaries—to scatter the seeds of a musical faith in a world not yet subdued to musical influences."

Many did embrace Tourjée's ideals, and America's musical life continued to expand, just as Tourjée so fervently wished.

EBEN TOURJÉE: THE LARGEST CONSERVATORY IN THE WORLD

2

It is harder to rule an orchestra than to govern New Jersey.

—*Eben Tourjée*

So Tourjée moved his Conservatory to the St. James Hotel in Franklin Square, trading the cramped, noisy rooms of the Music Hall for six stories of offices, dormitories, and rehearsal space.

At the time, the move seemed a good business decision. Tourjée wanted to expand; to do that, he needed to offer not only better musical facilities but accommodations where his students would be safe from "the whirl of the corrupt, brilliant life" of the big city. For his Conservatory was profoundly Christian and thoroughly female.

From his opening days, Tourjée relied on young women to keep his institution going. In its first year, 588 of the Conservatory's 719 registered students were women. And for the next thirty years, three out of every four of the students, and a still higher percentage of the most serious ones, were women. They were most strongly represented in piano and voice, the two largest and most profitable departments. Such numbers occasioned some heavy-handed humor among guests and trustees. When Boston's Mayor Hugh O'Brien visited NEC for dinner, he made awkward courtesies to the "young, handsome, and intelligent young ladies" who surrounded him. The Reverend Duryea, a longtime trustee and friend, began one lecture with the leaden joke that his audience should consider him "one of the girls"—since "girls are in the habit of talking."

Unlike such men, Tourjée saw a more serious side to women's education. He recognized that music provided women with an economic opportunity: with the proper training, they could teach either privately, in church choirs, or in schools. After the Civil War, teaching had become the most accessible career for women, promising both a profession and a measure of independence. The Conservatory tried to attract women by preaching the value of music as one of those "respectable"—and even marriageable—"accomplishments" that America's rising middle classes wanted. To them, it offered a finishing school for their daughters. That idea survived well into the twentieth century. Rose Kennedy (née Fitzgerald), for example, along with her sisters and cousins, attended the Conservatory for voice and piano lessons.

The St. James Hotel, located in the heart of the city, offered a "Cultured Home" for the five hundred women students and space for Tourjée's "Largest and Finest Conservatory in the World."

Rose Kennedy studied piano and voice, but her courtship, and later engagement, to Joseph P. Kennedy during her time at NEC took precedence.

In the 1880s and '90s, an unescorted woman on the streets of Boston was flirting with danger. Tourjée's Home offered safe protection for his "lady students."

As his Conservatory grew, Tourjée found himself with female students scattered all over town. He tried to find them suitable lodgings with local families, but such arrangements neither satisfied him nor reassured worried parents. He preferred to house and supervise them himself, one of his primary reasons for relocating to the St. James Hotel, only about ten blocks away from the Music Hall, on the corner of East Newton and St. James streets, in the South End. Built in 1868 and backed by a large open space, this imposing six-story brick and granite building fronted Franklin Square. Tourjée envisioned turning it into not only housing accommodations for the women but also a bustling musical center, the focus for his educational ambitions.

The St. James Hotel, circa 1890s

To pay for it, he convinced two Conservatory trustees, Eben Jordan, Sr., and Oliver Ditson, to guarantee the $1 million he needed. Then he sold his own home and took out a $250,000 mortgage to pay for two adjacent lots and renovations. The purchase gave him "The Largest and Finest Conservatory Building in the World," with ample space for classrooms, library, reading rooms, parlors, offices, and a museum of rare musical instruments. It offered the newest conveniences: two new Otis elevators, steam heat and laundry, hot and cold running water, a telephone, and even electric lighting—"the clear, beautiful light of the Edison lamp." And he advertised that this "splendid building, so magnificently equipped, is located in the heart of Boston—confessedly the musical and artistic center of America—and on one of the most desirable sites, where…the quiet of a home is combined with access to all the advantages of the city." With rooms for five hundred students, it made a "Cultured Home" for Tourjée's young ladies.

In his hyperbolic advertising, Tourjée extolled the practical advantages of young women's learning music. Despite a certain fondness for dilating upon the melancholy consequences of becoming a widow or going blind, he recognized that music offered one of the few opportunities for accomplishment, success, and even prestige that a woman might enjoy. So he loudly advertised that those opportunities were now available in America, arguing that young women no longer needed to brave the difficult and expensive passage to Europe, which he saw as nothing more than "the high road to perdition."

While Tourjée publicized the professional opportunities for women in music, he never forgot the moral character of his Conservatory. Even in the earliest days, while offering forty-cent lessons in the grimy Music Hall, he placed his women students with Christian families, providing not only inexpensive accommodations but reassurance for nervous parents. And at the first graduation ceremony, he seized the moment to denounce the idea of music "as a handmaid to vice" and enjoined each of his thirteen graduates to serve music as "a reformer, an educator, a symbol of all that is beautiful, noble, and good."

To attend his "500 lady students" in Franklin Square, he hired not only a preceptor and floor assistants but also women physicians and gym teachers. He moved his family into apartments on the sixth floor of the "Home"—as the former hotel was quickly dubbed—so that he could always be on hand. He required students to attend nondenominational chapel daily (and three times on Sundays), where he led them in traditional praise services, playing accompaniment on his small reed organ. He insisted on daily exercise and steered his students away from temptations of the flesh. He designated the first Tuesday of each month as a health day, when students were admonished to "eat only the purest foods, drink only the purest water." That emphasis on purity extended into the moral realm as well. When Oscar Wilde's *Lady Windemere's Fan* came to Boston, he barred Conservatory women from going to the theater, for fear that the comedy might remind them of its much-publicized author and his notorious private life. All was done, as Reverend Duryea proclaimed, so that the students would be "shielded as thoroughly as girls ever can be shielded in a great city."

For Tourjée, the Home's reputation constituted the Conservatory's primary concern. In 1888 newspapers published the scandalous story of young ladies walking Boston streets unescorted and addressing young men, then added the incriminating detail that many of them had rolls of sheet music in their hands. Tourjée hired private detectives to follow them and prove that they were not Conservatory students at all, but impostors, carrying sheet music as a cover for their "misbehavior."

Along with this typically Victorian concern for the moral life of his female students, he focused a more modern interest on their professional opportunities and political rights. Tourjée urged conductors and audiences to "make way for the ladies," adding that "some of us may live to see the day when a whole orchestra will be filled up with female performers." In that, he was woefully optimistic. But in all his publications, he urged not only the abilities of women but the opportunities they offered to music. And he had no truck with contemporary male educators who discovered in women a "receptive," rather than "creative,"

genius. That, he argued, was nonsense: "With women at last fairly entered into competition," he thought that "the coming generation may find a race of female composers, just as the present possesses a host of female executants." Although he did all he could to lure women students from piano and voice to other, neglected instruments, he nevertheless gloried in his school's "one particular star": the great diva from Maine, Nordica.

Nor did he blanch from the political implications of the women's place in the new generation. A longtime supporter of the YMCA, the Methodist Mission, and the Young Ladies' Missionary Society, he recognized that social and economic changes made women's education a necessity. As he told the Massachusetts legislature in 1889, the ideal of marriage was not even a possibility for the state's seventy-five thousand "redundant" women. Therefore, they had to learn to provide for themselves. In its own special field, the Conservatory taught them how to do that. Although it educated few international "stars," it trained a generation of self-supporting, independent music teachers. And when women's suffrage took the stage later on, Conservatory students and alumnae were quick to embrace "the Cause" as their own.

The Home provided safe, convenient, and inexpensive accommodations for five hundred Conservatory women. The $5 weekly fee for room and board was so reasonable that critics insisted he was foolish for not raising it to $7.50. But it also entailed two obligations that haunted Tourjée and hastened his collapse. First, he had to keep those five hundred beds filled and those six stories echoing with the

RECITATION ROOMS

MORNING READINGS

JOHNSON

SCHOOL OF
ELOCUTION
AND
DRAMATIC ART.

*Elocution and dramatic arts were added to
complete Tourjée's vision of a School of Music,
Literature, and Art.*

sounds of paying students. During its Music
Hall days, Conservatory enrollment had
fluctuated wildly. There were usually at least
one hundred more students in the winter
than in the summer: in 1871, for example,
735 registered for the winter, only 579 for the
summer term; in 1881, 771 and 634. The
problem was Tourjée's "special students,"
people who dropped by the Music Hall for a
lesson or two. The large numbers of these
students, and their fitful attendance, help
explain the phenomenally low graduate rates
of "the world's largest Conservatory."
In 1870, for example, only 13 of the school's
1,414 students graduated; in 1884, only 40
of 1,949; in 1887, 67 of 2,024.

To sustain full-time enrollments and
pay his bills, Tourjée turned the Conservatory into a "School of Music, Literature,
and Art." By 1886 he employed more than
one hundred teachers and administrators;
offered instruction in thirteen separate
schools, including ones for church music,
piano tuning, foreign languages, elocution,
fine arts, and "physical culture"; and
blanketed New England with advertisements
for "both class and private lessons." His
original mission—to provide cheap, efficient
music lessons through the class method—
was getting lost in the clutter of programs
whose purpose was solely to pay the bills.

Despite his success in attracting
students, Tourjée's hope of providing
an American musical education was also in
danger of compromise. Since his days
with the East Greenwich Academy, he had
schemed to construct an American
conservatory, insisting that the country's
"tuneful life" made it unnecessary for
Americans to get their musical education in
Europe. He had moved to Boston to
capitalize on the teaching talent there.
But now the cavernous halls of the St. James
Hotel needed more, and still more famous,
teachers. As *Dwight's Journal* had predicted,
"Nothing quiet, modest, small will answer;
we must do a big business." For that, the
Conservatory even relied on the very force
Dwight's Journal most despised: "The mod-
ern art of arts, the art of Advertising."

Vol. 6.   BOSTON, FEBRUARY,

Tourjée placed his faith in two great forces: God and advertising. Now he needed them both. To secure divine assistance, he incorporated his Conservatory in May 1883, transferring ownership to fifty trustees— including the Reverends Duryea, Hovey, and Muxom—and charged them "forever to maintain the institution as a Christian school of learning." For secular help, he flooded New England with flyers and posters, courted Boston's two dozen news-papers, and bought out the failing *Vox Humana*, reissuing it as the *Musical Herald*. "Dedicated to the Art Universal," the *Musical Herald* nevertheless heavily advertised the Conservatory local. For five years, it gave a running account of NEC's calendar, inclu-ding registrations, dinners, concerts, recitals, and reviews, all presented with an unfailing eye for praise and publicity.

Even in the Gilded Age, though, Tourjée had to have something to advertise. So he abandoned his more modest edu-cational ideas in favor of what even admirers called a "star system," importing such European luminaries as Augusto Rotoli, Carl Faelten, Leandro Campanari, and Emil Mahr. Their arrival in 1886 was not simply a signpost in the Conservatory's progress; it was a social event. Mahr, a talented French violinist, had toured with Madame Patti. Violinist Campanari, only twenty-eight when he arrived in Franklin Square, had debuted at age twelve. Faelten, the Saxon pianist, had enjoyed public association with composer Joachim Raff and the admired pianist Clara Schumann. Rotoli had conducted and sung at the funeral of Victor Emmanuel. Reviewing their accomplish-ments, Tourjée congratulated his institution for "drawing to itself the best European teachers of song, organ, and violin."

The Musical Herald,
the Conservatory's newspaper

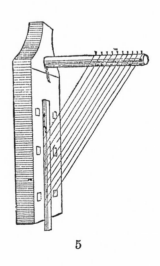

5

Their arrival, however, made NEC seem less an American music school than a music school in America. That marked a change in Tourjée's thinking. In his early days, he had argued that American teachers were as good as their European counterparts. Now he conceded that he had been mistaken. Struggling to meet ever higher musical standards, he bowed to European tradition, and so raised, once again, the question of what American music was to mean.

That question struck at the heart of Boston's musical culture. The year before, Wilhelm Gericke had dismissed twenty Boston musicians from the BSO, replacing them with musicians brought in from Vienna. Critics agreed that they worried the orchestra was becoming a musical version of the Red Sox: a group of players hired elsewhere, assembled in the city, and put before the local public without any real ties to Boston. Then, if they performed well, paying audiences hailed them as their own.

Tourjée, too, opted to "secure the services of some great European artist," rather than find an American. Those musical stars, though, complicated the life of the Conservatory. While their names adorned its larger and more frequent advertising, their contribution to the school was suspect. They were rarely in residence. Even Faelten complained that his European colleagues appeared only as "a sort of advertisement," then rushed off on concert tours, leaving the teaching to less well known—and less well paid—musicians. That created a rift that continued to trouble the Conservatory after Tourjée's death: the division between enthusiastic Americans with limited recognition and recently imported European stars.

Despite high enrollment and a star system, the heart of NEC's problem continued to be money. Like other entrepreneurs of the Gilded Age, Tourjée speculated on the future, throwing his school and his savings into the greatest gamble of his life. The St. James Hotel venture ended up requiring $1 million, with the cost of refitting, setting up rehearsal halls, and buying more than two hundred new pianos.

The new building even had a fatal weakness. Although it boasted a chapel, gymnasium, and bookstore, it lacked a recital hall. Students and their teachers played in the dining hall. Concerts were farmed out all over Boston. Even Tourjée, whose advertisements allowed only perfection, conceded the "real necessity of a hall for the general exercises of the institution." So he set about building one, despite facing two roadblocks: no room and no money. Tourjée wanted a comfortable hall, something between the 2,500-seat Music Hall and the old Minot or Chickering rooms, which sat barely a few hundred people. And he wanted a large stage, not simply for the piano and vocal recitals he advertised, but for the symphony orchestra he dreamed about. There was no room in his Conservatory for such a hall. Its long corridors and regular Georgian wings made digging out such a space impossible. Nor was there any money.

That did not stop Tourjée. His newly appointed trustees included some of Boston's most highly respected, and wealthiest, men. Richard Dana, Charles Gardner, Eben Jordan, Sr., and Rufus Frost, his board president—all brought social prestige and financial acumen to his enterprise, and he tapped them to raise still more money.

In 1884 he bought a half block of undeveloped land adjacent to the Conservatory from the city for twenty-eight cents a foot. He did not even have the money for that. Instead, he advertised for people willing to contribute the smallest sums in return for a kind of proprietary interest in a foot or two of the new space. Two larger contributions helped him realize his scheme. Rufus Frost chipped in $25,000. Jacob Sleeper, the aging financier who had helped found Boston University, gave another $10,000 and had the hall named for him.

Their generosity, along with another round of borrowing, financed Sleeper Hall. Built as quickly and as cheaply as Tourjée dared, the new hall opened on January 13, 1886, barely eighteen months after the land had been acquired. Tourjée advertised that, for "beauty and usefulness," his concert hall "o'ertops all other audience rooms of its kind, even here in Boston." It offered every modern convenience, including "the Tudor System of heat and ventilation," electric lighting, and a new organ. It also embodied that era's idea of beauty, with artistic frescoes, blue detailing, and heavy gilt embellishment.

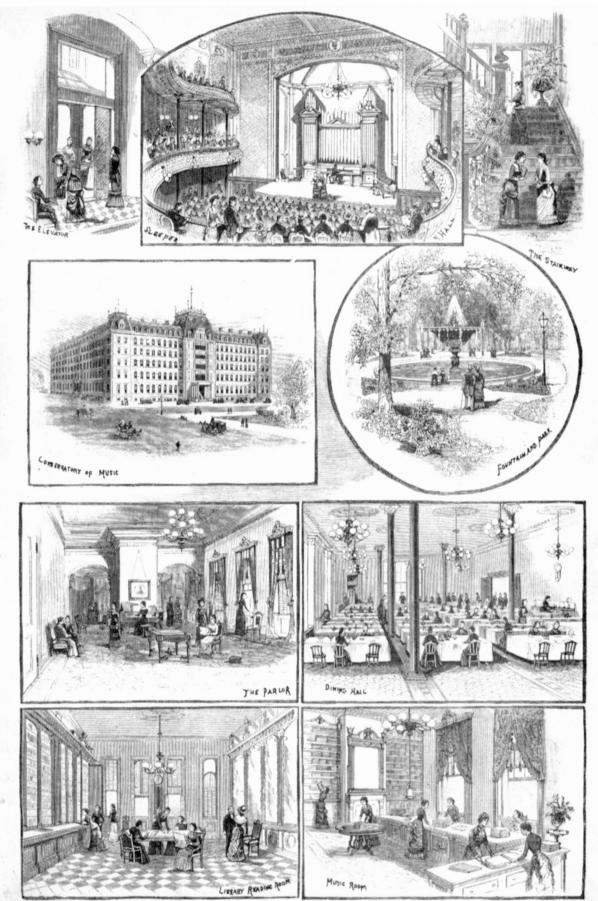

THE ELEVATOR

SLEEPER HALL

THE STAIRWAY

CONSERVATORY OF MUSIC

FOUNTAIN AND PARK

THE PARLOR

DINING HALL

LIBRARY READING ROOM

MUSIC ROOM

MASSACHUSETTS.—MUSICAL EDUCATION ON A GRAND SCALE—THE NEW ENGLAND CONSERVATORY OF MUSIC, BOSTON.
FROM SKETCHES BY C. UPHAM.

In words as artificial as the decorations, Louis Elson, the *Globe* music critic and Conservatory music history teacher, hailed the new hall:

O Art Divine, behold thy new-made dwelling:
Descend upon the altar which we raise!
While unto thee our homages are welling,
While in thy own pure tones is proudly
swelling
  Our song of praise.

But Sleeper Hall, like Elson's poem, fell short of perfection. It sat only 550 people, and most of them had to peer from the heavy balconies surrounding and dominating the stage. The stage itself, described as "ample," was in fact small. It supported the new organ, a recently purchased piano, and not much else. And while its acoustics were well suited to small groups and still smaller voices, its confined space, hemmed in by the balconies, amplified and distorted the sound of larger ensembles. At best, the new hall was an ornate compromise between what Tourjée wanted and what he could afford.

For all its failings, it was still a desperately needed addition to the Conservatory. In the first year, it accommodated 109 classical music concerts, 312 lectures, hundreds of student recitals, and, since Tourjée preferred it to the chapel, those 3 religious services every Sunday. It became the center of his work and the showplace for his visitors. Its dedication drew such political notables as Governor Robinson—who had never before visited NEC—former Governor Rice, and Mayor O'Brien. Four days later, on a Sunday, the famous but aged Reverend Phillips Brooks himself delivered the dedicatory sermon, a sure sign of Tourjée's acceptance by Boston's Brahmins.

Sleeper Hall's inaugural concert on January 21, 1886, showed off NEC's new musical connections as well, with performances by the school's brightest new European stars. Signor Rotoli sang Handel's *Sosarme* and his own *Mountain Song*. Campanari played Sarasate's *Romanza Andaluza*. Faelten not only performed Rubinstein's Second Etude but joined Timothée Adamowski—yet another of Tourjée's newly hired violinists—in Grieg's Sonata No. 2.

The hall, though, was as likely to stage a play or lecture as a concert. Students acted out their Shakespeare carnivals there. Drama teachers read Longfellow. Guest lecturers described their miscellaneous adventures in places like Alaska or Mexico, complete with newfangled stereopticons. Even suffragettes were allowed use of the hall to argue for the vote and to present showcases on "Women in History."

Wilhelm Gericke

Ignacy Paderewski

Sleeper Hall also gave Tourjée the
space he needed to host Conservatory guest
performers. He no longer had to ask them
to perform in a tangle of tables in the dining
hall. Before Sleeper had been completed,
he had entertained Wilhelm Gericke, newly
arrived as the BSO conductor, as well as
the renowned divas, Madame Amalie
Materna and Madame Birgit Nilsson. Each
had been gracious. Each had exclaimed over
the Conservatory's size and facilities. But
each had begged off the appeals to perform.
The addition of Sleeper Hall changed that.
When Helene Hastreiter, the prima donna
for the American Opera Company, visited in
May 1886, she climbed the new stage
and sang not only Gluck's *I Have Lost My
Eurydice* but also, to far livelier applause,
Foster's *Way Down upon the Swanee River*.
Franz Kneisel, Gericke's newly imported
concertmaster, played there in July. Ignacy
Paderewski, the charismatic Polish pianist,
performed in December—his already
famous long hair attracted at least as much
attention as his lively show. Mr. and Mrs.
George Henschel sang there for
Conservatory students in May 1887. He was
the former BSO conductor, composer of
note, and much-admired baritone, and she
was the former Lillian Bailey, with a voice
more widely admired than her husband's.
They were followed by the most distinguished of Boston's artistic and social
figures: on May 24 of that year, Dr. Oliver
Wendell Holmes—"The Autocrat of the
Breakfast Table"—read his poetry from the
intimate stage.

*Reflecting the nation's belief in the musical
superiority of Europeans, BSO director
Wilhelm Gericke replaced twenty Boston
musicians with twenty Viennese musicians.*

*Ignacy Paderewski, with his wild hair and
charismatic personality, was one of Sleeper
Hall's most exciting performers.*

Sleeper Hall further established the Conservatory's place on Boston's—and America's—musical stage. It provided a public forum for the school's talents, an advertisement for its place in musical culture, and a theater for its many friends. But for all its utility, the hall was already an anachronism. Built to stage piano and vocal recitals, it was inadequate for Tourjée's growing ambitions. Since 1872 he had dreamed of "the establishment in America of a vast UNIVERSITY OF MUSIC," with a real orchestra as its capstone. And despite Sleeper's shortcomings—its small size could not accommodate a full-scale orchestra—the long-lived scheme of offering "orchestral accompaniment" seemed about to be realized.

Major Higginson's commitment to a symphony orchestra, announced in 1881, had suggested that there was an audience for such music. Tourjée had pricked up his ears when Higginson added that "one more thing should come of this scheme, namely, a good, honest school for musicians." The time to form an NEC orchestra seemed favorable. So after moving into Franklin Square, he advertised for orchestra auditions. Only twenty-one students tried out for the new ensemble; nineteen of them played the flute.

That humiliation failed to deter him. In 1884 he jerry-rigged an orchestra, filled out by "our best resident artists," with faculty members J.B. Claus conducting and Henry Dunham substituting for the missing wind section on Sleeper Hall's organ. Desperately in need of wind and string players, Tourjée strengthened his string faculty by adding Campanari, Adamowski, and Mahr; reduced fees to two dollars a term for "boys on the violin"; and threw scholarships at wind players from across the country. Nothing worked: in the year he launched his orchestra, the Conservatory graduated only one violinist from an enrollment of 1,971. Eichberg's Boston Conservatory, though in its decline, still attracted the lion's share of the local string players, and Tourjée couldn't lure promising musicians from beyond Boston. NEC seemed destined to remain a school for piano and voice.

Louis Elson, the music history teacher, suggested trying to "tempt some of these young ladies to take up the bassoon, double bass or tuba" by offering "a bribe of a bouquet of flowers…chocolate caramels, or something of the kind." That idea was as far off the mark as his verses about Sleeper Hall. Despite the offer of flowers and candy, women students decided against orchestral instruments for practical reasons: piano and singing provided for a profession. Women singers like Patti, Melba, or the Conservatory's own Nordica commanded widespread public acclaim and as much as $2,500 an appearance. Women pianists like Adamowski's future wife, Antoinette Szumowska, performed in recitals or even as soloists with America's few symphony orchestras. For women of lesser talents, there were teaching positions, singing classes, private tutorials, or church jobs. For women who played string, wind, or reed instruments, however, there was little opportunity at all. Excluded from symphony orchestras, mistrusted by the deeply conservative musical establishment, and therefore at a decisive disadvantage even in offering lessons, they had few prospects for success. NEC faculty signaled that clearly: none of its seventeen women teachers offered instruction in orchestral instruments.

So Tourjée's orchestra limped on, a pampered collection of boys in a school for young women. He and Claus refused to give up. They convinced some thirty students to audition, then conducted rehearsals in the confines of Sleeper Hall. When they could not all fit on stage, Claus scattered them about the hall. Whole sections sat in the floor seats or balconies. Despite the difficulties, he succeeded in nursing a handful of public performances out of that first NEC orchestra. In March 1884 he led them through two movements of Haydn's Second Symphony; in May 1886 he conducted most of Mozart's Fifth Symphony. In between, he organized a handful of concerts and soirées that even Tourjée ignored, except to insist, against all odds, that the orchestra "has made rapid strides in the way of improvement."

In 1887, Tourjée admitted defeat. He shut down his ersatz orchestra, dismissed Claus, and ended his experiment. Recognizing that he lacked strings and wind instruments, rehearsal space, and even a hall large enough to accommodate symphonic sound, he was too shrewd—and too hard-pressed—an entrepreneur to throw good money after bad.

Tourjée faced the greatest financial crisis in the history of his underfunded institution. The Conservatory was in danger of going under. With an annual income of almost $250,000, it managed to meet regular expenses. Tourjée paid extraordinary ones out of his own pockets. But he was not able to pay off the mortgage on the St. James, which, by 1888, had ballooned to $800,000, and the trustees were forced to look for help.

They appealed to the state. Governor Robinson had spearheaded legislation providing $200,000 to the Institute of Technology, but it had only eight hundred students. His successor, Governor Ames, hinted that he might support similar assistance for the much larger Conservatory. So when NEC's trustees met in December 1888 to prepare their case, they decided to ask for $300,000 to help pay off accumulated debts and set the school's finances in order.

They began in traditional style. On January 23, 1889, Rufus Frost and his fellow trustees squired the governor through a dinner and concert in Franklin Square, climaxing with an organ recital of the hymns that Ames loved. The soloist was Wallace Goodrich, one of Henry Dunham's most promising students, whose career of Conservatory service continued for another fifty-four years. The dinner was merely a prelude: on February 9, the trustees, teachers, and Tourjée, armed with witnesses and statistics, descended on the State House to make their case.

For Tourjée, that was a final effort to save the great enterprise of his life. Not yet fifty-five, he looked far older; he already suffered recurrent headaches and frequent lapses of memory. Friends who had accompanied him on a recuperative trip to the West in 1886, and those who welcomed him back to his duties in 1887, recognized that he had not long to live. Now he called on his failing powers of persuasion and advertisement one more time, to make certain that when he died, his Conservatory did not go with him.

He brought three arguments to the State House. Harkening back to the days of Lowell Mason, he first tried to convince the rollicking, notoriously corrupt politicians of Massachusetts that his school played an important role in contemporary education. Parading his European stars, he emphasized the cultural accomplishments of his students and the growing place of music in America.

But he was shrewd enough to recognize how little that mattered. So he seconded his claim with a more practical assessment of his school's importance: it brought $20 million a year into the city. Unmoved by his appeal to their educational principles, committee members sat up at the prospect of revenue. They grilled him on the amount, his methods of calculating it, and, should the Conservatory fail, what might become of that money. They forced him to concede that his school, with 60 percent of the students coming from within the state, was far more local than he had advertised. And they hinted, perhaps mirroring their own experience, that some of the subsidy would go into his own pocket. Tourjée, who had put everything he owned into the Conservatory and had not even drawn a salary in years, found that allegation particularly galling. But he swallowed his pride and produced evidence to support his financial claims.

Finally, he brought in Miss Tobey, president of Massachusetts's rapidly growing Women's Christian Temperance Union. A formidable power in her own right, she testified that the Conservatory provided training and jobs for many of the state's struggling "redundant" women; without it, she feared they all too likely were to be drawn into saloons and—in the word of a gentler age—"sin." The WCTU, drawn almost exclusively from the churchgoing middle classes, knew little about prostitution or the women who were reduced to working at it. But Miss Tobey saw that the Conservatory provided training and jobs for women, and she threw her organization's support behind it.

The legislators were impressed. The raid on the state budget seemed to be going well. But Tourjée underestimated the opposition. He had argued that his Conservatory provided culture, training, and jobs for thousands of students every year. His critics brushed that aside. They attacked him for failing to produce international celebrities. They conceded the "eminence" of Lillian Norton and George Chadwick, whose *Melpomene* had been well reviewed by BSO audiences, but they insisted that the true test of a conservatory was its ability to produce a whole galaxy of stars, who "reflected the most light upon this country."

NEC failed that test. But so did every other musical institution in America. With only a handful of schools, two genuinely professional orchestras, and an aversion to serious music that bordered on perverse pride, the country was not likely to nurture the kind of talents that would impress parochial legislators. They wanted a fistful of American Paderewskis and Yankee Wagners, and they grew impatient when told it would take decades of serious work to produce them.

They also turned Tobey's argument and Tourjée's careful calculations against them. The state had given money to the Institute of Technology to subsidize future degree recipients who happened to be men; now it was asked to "do something for the young women." The school's dependence on special students and abysmal graduation rates were liabilities, but the politicians treated the idea of subsidizing education for women with the kind of high humor they felt it deserved. The subsidy was duly rejected.

Tourjée was heartbroken. Board members Rufus Frost and Richard Dana, who had helped prepare the appeal and thrown their prestige behind it, were deeply disappointed. There was nothing to do but

In Memoriam

✝

Eben Tourjée

try again. So in 1890 they marched back to the State House, repeated their earlier performance, and proved Marx's dictum that history repeats itself only as farce. The legislature, which had once been conscientious, was now bored and hostile. The press, which had reported the first effort with sympathy, sneered and derided the second. Even Tourjée's sometime friends weighed in against him. Leading the way was John Knowles Paine, first professor of music at Harvard, co-founder of the Harvard Musical Association, president of the Boston Orchestra Club, composer of *Oedipus Tyrannus*, and erstwhile composition teacher at the Conservatory. Paine was the most prestigious figure in Boston music. But he turned against his former employer and pushed the interests of Harvard, insisting that the education of performers, especially male performers, was better left to "established" schools.

Two years of appeal by Tourjée and his trustees not only failed to win help but diverted much-needed energy from other Conservatory projects. The *Musical Herald* closed down after seven years of incessant, but good-humored, promotion. Claus's orchestra, ragtag ensemble that it was, collapsed. Even the European stars, except for Adamowski and Faelten, left, ending the dream of making the Conservatory something more than a ladies' finishing school.

Clouded by age, failure, and a lifetime of hard work, Tourjée fell ill. The man who had simultaneously run the Conservatory, YMCA, North End Mission, *Musical Herald*, and National Music Teachers' Association, as well as various summer excursions, religious revivals, publishing, performance, and music festival enterprises, now found himself unable to work. His memory faded. His health, which had sustained an impossible schedule for two decades, gave way. In the summer of 1890, Conservatory employees found him dazed, unable to recognize them, and lost in the corridors of his vast white elephant. They helped him back to his sixth-floor apartment, put him to bed, and worried as his life drained slowly away.

Tuning Department

CARL FAELTEN:

EUROPEAN CUSTOMS

3

On April 12, 1891, Eben Tourjée, not yet fifty-seven, died. The Conservatory that had been his life's work—deeply in debt, unsure of its place in the musical culture, and with a divided faculty—seemed on the verge of a similar collapse. During the director's illness, the Conservatory's affairs had fallen into the hands of a directing committee: Henry Dunham, NEC alumnus and chairman of the organ department; Frank Hale, head of the Conservatory's tuning school as well as its business manager; and Carl Faelten. After Tourjée's death, Dunham and Hale nominated Faelten to lead the school, and the Board of Trustees unanimously accepted their choice. The new director moved upstairs, the obvious, but ill-fated, candidate of an institution looking (as Dunham sheepishly admitted) for "someone more capable as an educator."

Faelten was certainly that. Only forty-four, he nevertheless had already acquired impeccable credentials for his new job. After studying at the Weimar Conservatory, he had trained with the highly regarded composer Joachim Raff, then accompanied him and Clara Schumann to Frankfurt, where they spent five years building up the Hoch Conservatory. After Raff's death in 1882, Faelten had migrated to America and settled in Baltimore's Peabody Institute, where he strengthened its popular piano department.

He was an outstanding pianist as well as pedagogue. His first appearance in Boston, part of an 1884 barnstorming tour along the Eastern seaboard, won unanimous critical approval. His interpretation of Schumann's *Fantasie*, dedicated to Liszt and harkening back to his days in Frankfurt, was hailed for its "fire and vigor." On the strength of his acclaim, Tourjée had lured him away from the Peabody in 1885 and set him up as one of his three European "stars." In 1886 he not only played the first piano notes in Sleeper Hall, accompanying Timothée Adamowski in Grieg's Sonata No. 2, but also joined Wulf Fries in Boston's Chamber Music Society performances.

Professionally, Faelten was all the trustees needed. The new director, though, was a surprising choice for a school that had prided itself on its American identity. Born in Thuringia, he had attended Germany's finest schools and had even been wounded in its war against France. After his recovery, he went on to appear with Raff, the Schumanns, and a galaxy of stars, taking his notions of both pedagogy and performance from that tradition. As director, he declared that the new order in Franklin Square would be follow "the customs of Europe."

Frank Hale started the Conservatory's tuning program, promising women careers as tuners with a $1,000 annual salary.

Eben Tourjée was immortalized in this bronze bust.

He inherited a huge, chaotic rabbit warren of a place where distinguished musicians and part-time enthusiasts taught courses from music, piano tuning, teacher training, elocution, and oratory to sculpture, dance, and "original plastiques, posings, and tableaux." Despite all the advertisements about its growing numbers of advanced students, the Conservatory depended on its ability to offer, and even to anticipate, whatever might interest paying students for as little as five dollars a term. Tourjée's attempts to keep the dorm open had cost the Conservatory its musical identity. It was now in danger of becoming nothing more than a topsy-turvy "School of Music, Literature, and Art."

Carl Faelten turned the Conservatory upside down during his tenure as director, dismissing Tourjée's star musicians, feuding with faculty, and sending the school deeper into debt. His one accomplishment: introducing the Conservatory's first opera class.

Faelten recoiled from such chaos. He wanted to turn that maze of odd schools and occasional teachers into a real European conservatory. He began by breaking the Conservatory's link with Boston University, which Tourjée had capitalized on almost two decades earlier, and setting New England Conservatory on its own path. He discarded the amateurish "Tonic Sol-Fa" ear training for the more rigorous European solfeggio, thus upsetting poorly trained teachers and alarming less-enthusiastic students. He also rid the faculty of its few stars, the comets who streaked through the halls of Franklin Square on their way to more prestigious engagements.

One alumnus recalled the evils of that "star" system. His highly advertised instructor scheduled only two lessons for the term. In the first, he helpfully informed the young vocalist: "Your tongue sticks up in your mouth like a huge piece of beef; go home and get it down." By the time the enterprising singer had done so, he learned that his second lesson had been canceled. His teacher had skipped to Europe.

Faelten put an end to that. He severed ties with some of Boston's most prestigious musicians, including Carl Zerrahn, B.J. Lang, and Eugene Thayer, insisting on full-time teachers. To shore up the school's prestige, he turned—perhaps inevitably—to Europe. In 1891, he hired the great Italian pianist and composer, Ferruccio Busoni. Busoni had won the prestigious Rubinstein Competition in St. Petersburg the year before, and though he used his position at NEC as a base for touring the United States and Europe, he nevertheless added greatly to the school's national visibility.

Faelten also abandoned Tourjée's enthusiastic advertising in favor of more decorous, professional claims. In doing all that, he took advantage of two opportunities his predecessor had never enjoyed. First the Conservatory's local competitors, including Eichberg's Boston Conservatory, had dwindled into insignificance. Since his school continued to draw its students from New England, Faelten capitalized on a virtual monopoly of local talent. Secondly, and more important, he no longer needed the fitful presence of stars, because he had a whole new galaxy of teachers in the Boston Symphony Orchestra. The Boston Symphony Orchestra required that its musicians dedicate all their time to the orchestra. Higginson had agreed to only two outside occupations: they might play for the Handel & Haydn Society, and they could teach at New England Conservatory. So Faelten drew still closer to the BSO, cementing a bond that strengthened the school and buttressed the orchestra for a century.

Italian pianist and composer Ferruccio Busoni, hired by Carl Faelten in 1891. His prestigious reputation drew attention to the Conservatory.

The new director's own talents, however, lay in his own piano department, the school's largest program. He revamped it by starting a piano pedagogy class and insisting on stringent auditions. He not only sat in on those but also seized the opportunity to snatch the best students for himself, reducing his colleagues to teaching the poorly prepared, amateurish remnants.

Faelten compounded faculty animosity by feuding with Frank Hale, the gregarious Yankee entrepreneur whom Tourjée had brought in to teach pianoforte and organ tuning. An amateur musical technician in a school of aspiring artists, Hale had his priorities clear: he advertised heavily (though not always accurately) that he trained tuners, including women, for jobs that paid the heady wages of $1,000 a year. No one better than Hale epitomized the catch-as-catch-can character of Tourjée's years. After coming to the Conservatory in 1880 to organize its tuning program, then (along with his brother Edward) teaching in the theory department, Hale ended his Conservatory career as its business manager. He had worked closely with the first director. Now he watched as the German pianist redirected Tourjée's great enterprise.

The new director could fend off exasperated colleagues, but for all his musical and educational accomplishments, Faelten lacked Tourjée's entrepreneurial sense. For a school already deeply in debt, that threatened disaster. He dutifully begged the trustees for $165,000 to ward off the school's creditors and even managed to nurse a small profit in 1895. But that was the first, and last, profit he was ever to see.

Faelten's changes gradually improved the quality of the school's musical education. He not only reformed the piano classes, strengthened the theory department, and attracted more gifted students, but also introduced the Conservatory's "class for operatic study" in November 1896. Taught by Max Hirschfeld, the man behind Boston's Castle Square Opera Company, it was the first of many efforts to give voice to the school's operatic ambitions. Faelten also won prestigious endorsements. In November 1893, Amy Beach, America's foremost female composer and celebrated figure of Boston society, testified to the "high standard of education" New England Conservatory offered the next generation of composers. She also celebrated the Conservatory's education of women.

In a number of personal appearances, some of music's brightest lights seconded Beach's opinion. In April 1895, Madame Melba, the greatest diva of the era, sang for Conservatory students. Already famous enough to have both a biscuit and dessert named for her, the Australian native sang Mimi in a way that haunted a generation of *La Bohème* enthusiasts, and dominated grand opera for a quarter of a century. The students loved her. And they loved Paderewski. The great Polish pianist had first displayed his prodigious talents, and that beautifully coifed hair, in Sleeper Hall in 1886; he performed there twice more under Faelten's regime. In December 1895 he gave a remarkable ninety-minute recital, the emotional highlight of a tour that brought him unprecedented public acclaim and $200,000 in profits. He was followed by the less charismatic, but equally talented, Emile Sauret, the masterful French violinist whose powerful performance in 1896 hushed Sleeper Hall and the dwindling number of violin students there.

Curriculum changes, critical endorsements, and personal appearances provided growing evidence of the new director's efforts at enhancing the quality and reputation of the Conservatory. But Faelten, like so many of his successors, came to grief over finances. Enrollment fell steadily, year by inexorable year. In the fall of 1890, NEC had registered 1,201 students; in 1893, 1,004; in 1896, 950. To some extent, Faelten's improvements seemed to work: the piano department did not shrink as fast as some of the others. In 1889, Tourjée had enrolled 702 pianists; five years later, Faelten still brought in 688. But Tourjée had also registered 328 voice students; Faelten could find only 241. And using advertisements for "cheap lessons at $2 a term," the founder had lured 169 "boys on the violin" into his string department. Faelten's tuition increases and compulsory solfeggio left him with only 17.

In April 1895, diva Madame Melba sang for the Conservatory in a performance that thrilled students.

The heavily mortgaged Home had to be filled to the rafters to pay its way, and Faelten, with his commitment to European standards, could not manage that. His changes not only cost the school much-needed revenues but also forced it to abandon once again the dream of launching a real Conservatory orchestra. In part, the times were to blame. By the mid-1890s, America was locked in the longest depression it had yet seen. Young people sought work, rather than accomplishments. The market for sheet music, concert tickets, and music teachers slumped, while Faelten insisted upon a professionalism the Conservatory could ill afford. Its teachers, perplexed by growing financial difficulties and personal grievances, grew angry. "If Faelten were to resign," Hale muttered, "the faculty would throw their hats in the air."

But Faelten stayed, and teachers continued to complain. That made matters worse. Disciplined, methodical, and easily angered, even in the best of times, the director turned suspicious and arrogant, alternately spying on faculty and staff, intimidating alumni, and boasting that he "had the Board of Trustees in his pocket." His behavior cost him the trust of the school's faculty, the support of its graduates, the confidence of its trustees, and finally his position as director. His fall began with complaints about his habit of poaching the best pianists. Charles Denée, a loyal alumnus whose daughter attended the Conservatory, and Carl Baermann, widely regarded as the most distinguished pianist in Boston, complained that they were unfairly losing students. Hale, watching the ledgers slide into the red, expressed his sympathy. In 1896, eighteen teachers, led by members of Faelten's own piano department, went over his head, appealing to the trustees to curtail his powers.

Their petition put the board's president on the spot. Son of the author of *Two Years Before the Mast* and heir to his family's rich philanthropic tradition, Richard Henry Dana, Jr., had reluctantly accepted the presidency in 1891. Like his father, who had suffered wounding accusations of plagiarism, he was a proud, reticent Boston gentleman, loathe to any public display of private quarrels. So his first instinct was to patch together a truce: he offered the eighteen teachers an indemnity against retribution but also gave the director an unqualified endorsement.

Faelten mistook Dana's accommodation for weakness and moved to make himself master of the Conservatory. Less than a week after the cease-fire, he swooped down on the dissidents and fired seven of them for dining together at the Clark Hotel. That threw the Conservatory into chaos. Dana, once again, stepped in. Even after learning of Faelten's paranoid reprisals, he tried to retrieve a kind of gentlemen's agreement. He offered to rehire several of the teachers, further investigate their charges, and lay the matter before the Board of Trustees. But in public, he continued to maintain that Faelten was not at fault.

Old hands at Franklin Square, however, knew otherwise. For Faelten's feud with the faculty quickly escalated into a campaign against the alumni. In June 1896, angered by its support for the teachers, he declared war on the Alumni Association.

He fielded his own candidates for its executive elections, then threw his formidable organizing talents behind them. His inexplicable urge to attack the association transformed a traditionally good-humored and ill-attended social gathering into a plebiscite on his years as director.

It also proved another of Faelten's mistakes, for the odds were stacked against him. Not only were the Alumni Association's popular officers standing for re-election, but the rank and file included many of the very teachers who had opposed him: Harry Redmon, one of Tourjée's last appointments; Henry Dunham, the popular head of the organ department; Hale; and the theory department's brightest light, George Whitefield Chadwick. Together, they rallied the opposition and turned back Faelten's assault on the Association officers.

In January 1897 they presented their own account of the Conservatory's troubles at the annual meeting of trustees. Dana, who now learned of Faelten's boast that he "had the Board of Trustees in his pocket," agreed to appoint a special committee to investigate, headed by the highly respected Reverend Alvah Hovey. On February 17, Hovey reported back to the board, finding enough substance in the accusations to advise against renewing the director's contract.

Faelten had his own code of honor, tied to the European ideas of dignity and courage. He lived up to its demands. After politely hearing out the committee report, he promptly resigned. Less than five hours later, after being humiliated, dismissed, and held responsible for the recriminations at his school, he appeared in Sleeper Hall to accompany Mary Patterson, one of the advanced students he had claimed as his own. Together they played Beethoven's Sonata in F-sharp Major for Pianoforte. The audience, already aware of his resignation, twice gave Faelten a standing ovation. He bowed in silent acknowledgment and, declining to comment, left the hall, never to return.

GEORGE WHITEFIELD CHADWICK: UNANIMOUS CHOICE

4

Your hotels are the wonder of the world,
your electric signs the despair of Europe,
your shops, your little town—many, many
things you do are marvels of thoroughness.
But in music—well.
  — *Enrico Caruso*, America's Musical Future

Even as Faelten stalked out, President Dana
was waiting in the wings. He and his fellow
trustees had already consulted with both
alumni leaders and disgruntled faculty.
Now, he stepped out onto Sleeper stage and
named the school's new director.

Their unanimous choice: George
Whitefield Chadwick. Even Faelten had
voted for him. At forty-two, he was already a
Conservatory veteran, first studying there
with George Whiting and Stephen Emery,
then returning to teach in its theory department. For the last fifteen years, as the
abortive appeals to the state in 1889 and 1890
had shown all too clearly, he had been
one of only two stars in the NEC firmament.

Despite the inadequate Sleeper Hall and the
lack of string players, Chadwick perserverved
in forging an orchestra out of nothing. By the
time Jordan Hall at NEC *was built, the* NEC
Orchestra had grown considerably.

Trustees were impressed by his Yankee
heritage and New England business sense. A
lifelong member of the Sons of the
American Revolution, he gloried in his
great-grandfather's appearance at the Battle
of Bunker Hill and his brother's commission
at Bull Run. The family's insurance
business had taken them from the mills
of Lowell to the genteel precincts of Boston's
new Back Bay. Chadwick had worked in
his father's office for less than a year, but he
had the look of an entrepreneur from some
Henry James novel: a stocky, serious figure,
with an open face, penetrating eyes, and
a slightly straggling mustache, he studiously
avoided the sartorial eccentricities
for which musicians were already famous.
Instead, he wore the ubiquitous business suit
of his age with a starched collar that was,
even then, slightly old-fashioned. And across
his businessman's vest, he wore the
era's most conspicuous symbol of success: a
weighty gold watch chain.

To the public, his selection offered
not only reassurance but promise. Too much
the Yankee to be confused with a man
like Faelten, he was too conspicuously
a musician to be taken for another Tourjée.
After leaving the Conservatory, he had
accepted a teaching job at Olivet College,
then gone to Europe for three years,
studying with Salomon Jadassohn in Leipzig
and Josef Rheinberger in Munich. Returning
to Boston in 1880, he had conquered the
local musical world: the Handel & Haydn
Society performed his *Rip Van Winkle*
Overture; the Philharmonic Society debuted
his *Beautiful Munich* waltz; the Harvard
Musical Association, his First Symphony.
His success carried over into more intimate
musical circles: the Arlington Club gave
the premier performance of his *Marguerita*,
while the Apollo Club staged his
Viking's Last Voyage. And in 1887 the Boston
Symphony Orchestra premiered his
romantic overture *Melpomene* to critical and
popular applause.

His reputation had already spread
far beyond Boston. In 1892 organizers of the
World's Columbian Exposition—better
known as the Chicago's World Fair—
commissioned him to write their inaugural
music. Like the Peace Jubilees before it, the
fair was less a cultural event than a circus,

George Whitefield Chadwick: his long Conservatory history as student and faculty and his impressive musical talent made him the unanimous choice to replace the ousted Carl Faelten.

but Chadwick responded to the challenge. He produced a three-movement *Ode* for an orchestra of five hundred, a chorus of five thousand, and three brass bands. It was a loud, garish piece, worthy of its occasion. It introduced Chadwick to a national audience, although his success was over-shadowed by the fair's better-known contribution to American culture: the hot dog. In 1894 a celebrity panel headed by Antonín Dvořák confirmed his success, awarding its grand prize to his Third Symphony. Chadwick took the award in stride. He told his friend, the conductor Theodore Thomas, that it meant his symphony would be "roundly abused by the newspaper reptiles in this town."

Thus, Chadwick came to his position as director with the reputation as the leading young American composer. When Philip Hale, the famous critic, described one of his musical compositions as representing "a certain jaunty irreverence, a snapping of the fingers at Fate and the Universe," he also called attention to the leading characteristic of the composer himself. He was a classicist, and his music was "notable for its fluency and beauty of rhythmic and melodic inventiveness, mastery of part-writing, its logical and coherent grasp of form." Yet, while indebted to German models, his work was recognizably American. His Third Symphony, for example, shared its key with Brahms's, but in place of Brahms's "Central European gravities," Chadwick was relaxed. As one reviewer wrote, Chadwick was "Brahms with his beard shaved off and grinning from ear to ear."

He was poised to succeed John Knowles Paine as the dean of American music. His *Harmony,* composed in 1897, became the standard text for a generation, going through seventy-four editions. He hobnobbed with Boston's musical lights, including not only Paine but John Dwight and B.J. Lang from the old guard, as well as Arthur Foote and Arthur Shepherd from the new. He trained a coterie of students who were to dominate the next generation of music, including Wallace Goodrich, Edward Burlingame Hill, Mabel Wheeler Daniels, and Frederick Converse. He also won the respect of Higginson's German professionals: he dedicated *Melpomene* to Wilhelm Gericke, who conducted it six times during his tenure with the BSO; he wrote his Quartet No. 3 for Franz Kneisel, Gericke's concertmaster; and he invited Timothée Adamowski to introduce his Quartet No. 5.

Chadwick seemed the ideal choice for a floundering Conservatory. Yet behind his musical accomplishments there lay a weakness he never forgot: he had none of the credentials for the work he was pursuing with such success. Although he clubbed with such sons of Harvard as Converse, Hill, and Walter Piston (as well as Radcliffe daughters like Daniels), he had grown up without their money or status. His family had made its fortune late. Even in Germany he had lived in poverty to pursue his studies. Over the course of his career, he received honorary degrees from Yale, Tufts, and Wisconsin universities, membership in the American Academy of Arts and Letters, and decorations from the National Institute of Arts and Letters. But he actually was a high school dropout. He had never even taken a diploma at NEC—the school he was to lead for thirty-three years.

Frederick Converse, one of Chadwick's prized students, took his mentor's distinctly American style into the next generation, as did other NEC students Wallace Goodrich, Edward Burlingame Hill, and Mabel Wheeler Daniels.

Chadwick was a self-made man. Born nine years before Henry Ford and seven years after Thomas Edison, he shared their circumstances and outlook. Too young to serve in the Civil War, they had all grown up in the heroic industrial days of the Gilded Age, when mushrooming cities offered unimaginable opportunities to shrewd, undereducated boys from the countryside. As they grew into leaders, they watched America change, its opportunities becoming more exclusively the preserves of professionals and pedagogues. Edison responded by denouncing the new generation of college-trained managers as "ninny philosophy students." Ford insisted that history— and anything else he could not understand —was "bunk." Chadwick shared their terse style and their distrust of the new order. Reversing Shaw's adage, he said all his life, "If you can play, you can teach."

But Chadwick could not play—at least, not very well. He had come to the keyboard late in adolescence and never mastered its intricacies. Just as Edison was a tinkerer, rather than a scientist, and Ford a salesman, rather than an engineer, Chadwick was a church organist, rather than a musician. Good enough to play in Boston's Park Street or Columbus Avenue Universalist churches, he never managed anything like Faelten's credentials or assurance in performance. Even at the peak of his career, he rarely accompanied anything except his own music. And his conducting career was confined almost entirely within the walls of the Conservatory, with only occasional dashes outside to wave the baton for his own work.

He consented to replace Faelten as director only when the trustees agreed that he wouldn't "have to give up [his] composing or conducting on account of it, otherwise [he] would not have accepted the place." Yet he wasn't universally welcomed: the New York–based *Musical Courier* dismissed his compositions, queried his $6,000 salary, and ridiculed his attempts to shape the NEC Orchestra, "as it is humorously called."

Chadwick understood the measure of American success. "We want to get money. We want to get rich," he told a convention of the National Music Teachers' Association. But he detested the most obvious route to such success: popular music. Joining battle with George Root, whose "Rosalie, the Prairie Flower" had earned $3,000, he denounced "this trash, this dishonest, inartistic, miserable stuff" so resoundingly that he later admitted he had spoken "perhaps too much in earnest," as close as he ever came to an apology.

He proffered advice with the confidence of a self-made man. He told students to pursue music as either an art or a business, though he suspected that many of them merely "preferred [it] to honest manual labor, for which they are really much better adapted." He echoed the social Darwinism of his day, announcing that musical education's one "laudable object" was "the suppression of the unfit." And he enforced the highest standards: "I do not ask you to make popular music classical," he told every educator he could find. "I ask you to make classical music popular."

This, then, was the successor to Tourjée and Faelten. Even among his closest friends, Chadwick was notorious for his brusque humor, sense of purpose, and habit of plain speaking. To his students, he was an alarming icon of Boston culture. He told one intimidated student from Illinois, "That's a good part of the country to be from—and get out of." He obeyed no will but his own: once, when he wanted some sheet music from the Conservatory's music room, he simply smashed the glass and took it. And he told his colleagues, with some relish, that his purpose was "to make war most energetically upon all frauds, all shams, all false teachers and teaching…and upon all false prophets."

He arrived at a critical moment in the Conservatory's history. Tourjée had come to Boston in the salad days of the amateur, when college orchestras and musical clubs played, as *Dwight's Journal* complained, "to a few handfuls of aesthetic Boston ladies of both sexes." Professional musicians were rare: there were only three hundred in all of Boston, only fifteen hundred in New York. They eked out a precarious living by playing for occasional orchestras, waltz parties, and dances in "lager-beer saloons." Tourjée had provided haphazard lessons for the city's amateur enthusiasts, while giving serious musicians work outside those saloons. His Conservatory was a small part of a great cultural awakening; a newly enriched, powerful, and astonishingly arrogant America suddenly demanded not only its own literature, art, and music but the best that its great wads of money could buy.

By the time Faelten arrived, those who promised to provide all that were earning salaries of $10,000, and Major Higginson had pledged $50,000 a year to the success of his new orchestra. Such sums brought a quality of music that had been unthinkable only a decade earlier. But it also professionalized music: amateurs were transformed from players into audiences, and such Boston institutions as the Harvard Musical Association, the Philharmonic Society, and even the Handel & Haydn Society withered in the face of this new professional competition. The Conservatory had to find a way to train those new professionals, or else it would dwindle into yet another finishing school.

Chadwick began his work by consolidating his predecessors' innovations. In his first full term, he resumed Tourjée's ill-fated efforts to establish a real orchestra. He met the same problems—too few strings and reeds, too little room—but refused to admit defeat. His first auditions produced fewer than thirty students, almost all of them violinists, so he lumped them together, put them in front of the organ, and began rehearsals. When Sleeper Hall proved too small for even that tiny band, he sent the second violins into the balconies and kept rehearsing. When he finally rounded up a couple of reed players, he used the organ to fill in for missing horns, then rehearsed his crew twice a week for eight months. On April 21, 1898 (perhaps fortuitously, while attention was focused on the opening days of the Spanish-American War), he sent his volunteers onto Sleeper's stage to try their luck at Handel's *Concerto Grosso*.

Handel proved too much for them. With the players scattered on stage and balcony, they never managed to find the same note at the same time. It was a humiliating failure, but it was a performance. Chadwick had marched his musicians onto the stage and balcony to take their licking; now he marched them back to rehearsals. Tourjée had listened to the performances of 1884–86, looked at Sleeper Hall, and admitted defeat. Chadwick heard the same noise, saw the same impediments, and resolved to continue.

For the immediate future, however, there were to be no more performances. Instead, Chadwick drove his charges through three years of rehearsals, bullying and begging them twice a week. By 1901 his string band had become something like an orchestra. His musicians now included some reeds and horns, though he had to hire oboes and bassoons to get the sound he wanted.

The first performance of Chadwick's orchestra was the Conservatory's 1901 Commencement concert in Tremont Temple. By 1903 the NEC Orchestra had taken its place in Jordan Hall at NEC.

In October 1901 he filed his orchestra back into the limelight. Forty students climbed onto Sleeper's stage and balcony to play Beethoven's *Overture to Egmont* and Haydn's Symphony in D. It was, as the director carefully warned, only a public rehearsal, but it prepared his musicians, and their audience, for a later performance on March 2, 1902, when Chadwick took the baton and led his students through the friendly movements of *Egmont*. On June 18, he conducted a commencement concert, braving an audience of seventy graduates, parents, alumni, and trustees. Since the ceremony took place in Tremont Temple, he even managed to get his entire orchestra performing together for the first time after five years of rehearsals. To celebrate the occasion, they worked their way through the opening movement of Rheinberger's Concerto in F—for the conductor, both a tribute to an old teacher and a shrewd calculation that a piece so traditionally arranged, so precise, and so routine would neither disappoint his audience nor alarm his nervous crew. The NEC Orchestra had tentatively announced its arrival.

The orchestra was only one of Chadwick's new projects. He also wanted opera, which was enjoying a boom in prosperous America. Enough traveling companies abounded to convince enthusiasts that with more money, or less expensive prima donnas, or bigger theaters, or more (or less) Wagner, the nation might find the artistry and audience for national opera companies. In Boston such sentiments had swelled in 1897–88, when Kahn's Metropolitan Opera and Hammerstein's Manhattan Opera companies had swept in from New York. They imported stars and scenery. Dozens of competing productions rang out from the Music Hall and Tremont Temple, including "all of Wagner's operas that hold the stage." Unkind critics pointed out that attendance peaked on "the non-Wagner nights" but agreed that opera was a hit with Boston's sophisticated audiences.

Signor Oreste Bimboni, former conductor of the Moscow Imperial Opera, swept into NEC at Chadwick's request and started the Conservatory's first opera program in 1901. Although he managed to stage a few productions in the old Boston Theatre, the program failed after only a few years.

In 1896, Faelten had tried to establish opera at NEC. Where he failed, Chadwick plunged in. In October 1901 he launched NEC's second voyage onto opera's troubled seas, hiring Signor Oreste Bimboni, former conductor of Moscow's Imperial Opera, the Vienna Imperial Opera House, and the Chicago Festival. Bimboni set sail for Boston immediately.

The patrician Yankee and cosmopolitan Italian made an unlikely pair of opera champions. Chadwick's musical world was dominated by a classicism that was already academic and even ironic. His themes came out of Greek literature, as Thalia, Adonais, and Euterpe suggest. Bimboni, on the other hand, was as florid as his new boss was conservative. He had careened all over the world, twice joined in Garibaldi's military escapades, and produced some of the most modern pieces in opera.

Their temperamental differences, however, paled in comparison to the obstacles they faced. Chadwick had spent the last three years chafing against the confines of Sleeper's stage. Now he hired Bimboni to try his hand with an orchestra, scenery, and actors crowding the same tiny space. The impresario sidestepped, rather than solved the problem: he never used Sleeper Hall, and he never produced an opera.

Instead, he moved his shows into the old Boston Theatre and relied on miscellaneous scenes to train his singers. In May 1902 he staged his first display: a handful of songs that began with the prologue of Gounod's *Faust,* then ran through various moments from *Lohengrin* and *La Traviata* before ending with the death scene from *Aïda*—an unabashed play for the sympathies of the audience. Boston's press resolutely ignored the affair, while the Conservatory's new *Magazine* admitted that "one or two slight mishaps occurred." In March 1903, Bimboni returned, offering tidbits from Meyerbeer, Verdi, Gluck, and Rossini, as well as a song from his own unproduced *La Modella.* In June he presented a third recital, with students singing excerpts from the inevitable *Aïda, Carmen,* and the final act of *Faust.* He concluded by promising to produce a full opera in the near future, modestly suggesting his own *Modella.* An opera school followed. Sustained by Bimboni's enthusiasm, it sank in the wake of his death in 1906. He had not been a conspicuous success: in the five years at NEC he had never put on a complete performance. So it was a curious valedictory when on May 18, 1906, Wallace Goodrich took the podium and conducted Ignaz Brüll's *Golden Cross:* NEC's first full opera. Bimboni's former assistant, Clayton Gilbert, directed the production.

Chadwick launched the school's first chorus in 1898, in hopes of performing such projects as Beethoven's Ninth Symphony or one of the endless oratorios that attracted contemporary composers. His standards were modest: "Everybody can sing," he claimed, "although there are many voices that were not intended by the Creator to give pleasure to others." But his chorus survived only a few years before Chadwick was forced to concede that he lacked the voices, the dedication, and the space to pull off ambitious pieces. Another generation would pass before the Conservatory could train enough good voices to establish a chorus to complement its orchestra.

Orchestra and opera added luster to the Conservatory, but they also highlighted the limits of Franklin Square. Chadwick hated everything about the old St. James Hotel, from its huge dormitory to its tiny hall. He hated the commitment to housing five hundred young ladies. He hated the financial worries that came with its mortgage, and he hated the neighborhood that was now attracting transients and boarders, rather than socialites and professionals. He wanted a real Conservatory, with practice rooms, recital halls, a full-size, versatile auditorium, and—as he frequently muttered—"no dormitories." He wanted a place to show off his fledgling orchestra, to strengthen his opera school, and to resuscitate his failed chorus. He wanted a new school. To get it, all he needed was land, money, and musicians.

EBEN JORDAN, 2ND: PARTNER IN A MODERN CONSERVATORY

5

In this new work, Chadwick had an important ally among the trustees. The Faelten fiasco had shaken not only faculty and alumni but the Conservatory corporation. Richard Dana, who hated publicity, had had enough. In 1898 he retired as president, succeeded by Charles Gardner. But the real force on the new Board of Trustees was Eben Dyer Jordan, 2nd. The eldest son of Boston's most famous retailer, Jordan was then—and remains—an enigmatic figure. A classmate of Teddy Roosevelt at Harvard, partner in Jordan Marsh, and amateur musician, he was quiet, even retiring. His diffidence hid a generosity that was to help shape decisively Chadwick's—and the Conservatory's—future.

Jordan Hall at NEC, with its superb acoustics, intimate stage, and classical architecture, became the Conservatory's musical heart.

That had not been clear when he reluctantly joined the board in 1895. Only thirty-eight, he was torn between a determination to continue his father's work and a fear of wasting his time. For Jordan Sr.— the man who had coined and advertised the slogan "the customer is always right"—had lived out an American story worthy of his contemporary, Horatio Alger. Arriving from rural Maine with a fortune variously estimated at anywhere from ten to twenty-five cents, he had worked, saved, and advertised his way to wealth. His Jordan Marsh department store had taken advantage of new European styles, a growing popular press, and the rising generation of middle-class consumers by providing the latest fashions at reasonable prices—with much-publicized sales—offered by knowledgeable, efficient, and polite employees.

They had good reason to be. Jordan Sr. had decided not only to treat his customers well—another of his heavily advertised slogans was "satisfaction guaranteed"—but to do the same for his employees. He paid better than prevailing wages, provided clean, comfortable working conditions, offered recreation and education for anyone interested, and even organized vacation trips at impossibly reduced fares. He found, much to the surprise and chagrin of his fellow merchants, that he did well by doing good.

During the 1869 Peace Jubilee, he also found Eben Tourjée. The two had much in common. Both lived outside the narrow confines of Boston society. Both were deeply committed to old-time Protestantism in a city dominated by Unitarianism. And both were philanthropists, throwing themselves into missionary schemes, soup kitchens, and the YMCA. So Jordan drew closer to the Conservatory, first advertising in its *Musical Herald*, then contributing to its appeals, and finally, in 1891, agreeing to serve on its Board of Trustees. He proved a diligent, rather than dominant, member, following along in the wake of Presidents Frost and Dana. When he died in 1895, his fellow trustees asked his son to take up the vacant chair as a courtesy to his father.

When Jordan joined the Board of Trustees, he was disconcerted by the condition of the Conservatory. It was adrift. To give it direction, he had personally appealed to Chadwick's studio and urged him to take on the directorship. Chadwick demurred, but Jordan persisted, promising a free hand in every aspect of Conservatory life. Overwhelmed by the offer, Chadwick reluctantly agreed to take the job. And so began the partnership that was to reshape NEC as a national conservatory of music.

Jordan Jr. and Chadwick became as close as Jordan Sr. and Tourjée had been, though for wildly different reasons. Both were Bostonians, part of the social world their predecessors had admired only from afar. Both were thoroughly conventional figures: the dark business suits, high-button vests, and starched stand-up collars they wore, along with their short hair, neatly trimmed whiskers, and modest mustaches, were uniforms of the respectable clan. Yet both were musical enthusiasts, with ambitions that seemed outlandish to the old guard. Both were also notoriously taciturn:

Chadwick had a penchant for brutal humor and plain talk; Jordan, for disconcerting seriousness and silence. Their stern sense of propriety and their thoroughly Bostonian ways alarmed students, teachers, and not a few trustees. But together they remade the Conservatory.

They worked from the ground up. In May 1901 they announced that they had deeded the St. James to Reverend George Perin. Their school was going to follow the BSO out to Huntington Avenue. Perin hoped to operate Boston's largest hotel for women. Chadwick was determined to get out of that line of work.

The design for the new school embodied his ideas of a modern Conservatory. There were, as he had promised, no dormitories in the building. Instead, three residential units, named after the school's first presidents, were built around the corner on Hemenway Street. The new Conservatory building was a model of classical architecture. Its severe facade and modest Doric entrance echoed Chadwick's fondness for the Greek tradition. The architect, Edmund Wheelwright of Wheelwright and Haven, was already the talk of Boston for his work with McKim, Mead, & White on Symphony Hall. The new building also added to the cultural district, which would eventually extend from Horticultural Hall to the Isabella Stewart Gardner Museum.

The building's new facade echoed Symphony Hall, although its interior was utterly different. Symphony Hall's antechambers led inexorably into its Palladian-style auditorium. The new Conservatory, on the other hand, offered four floors of corridors that circled the building, opening into classes, practice rooms, offices, a library, a bookstore, and even a faculty lounge. At its heart was a new hall with a large, versatile stage, big enough to seat an orchestra or stage an opera yet small enough to shelter a vocal recital or string quartet. Approximately eleven hundred people could be seated close enough to the stage to make each gesture and sound an intimate one. In every sense, the Conservatory was to be built around this musical heart, which was to be called Jordan Hall at NEC.

Jordan and Chadwick kept the project close to their chests but carried it through with speed and decision. By the time Boston learned of the scheme, they had acquired the property, approved Wheelwright's designs, and prepared for construction. Only a year after the BSO had moved to Huntington Avenue, the Conservatory began work on its new home just down the street.

Construction did not go well. Boston, like the rest of America, had finally shaken off the effects of the 1893 depression. The city was booming, as Brahmins put up their elegant and understated Back Bay mansions, Isabella Stewart Gardner built her own startling home in the Fens, and the less-prosperous middle classes threw up block after block of the new triple deckers, turning Roxbury, Dorchester, Somerville, and Cambridge into streetcar suburbs. New trams and trolleys radiated out to the rural world of Brookline, Newton, and West Roxbury. The trolley line along Huntington Avenue, already notorious for its noise and tremors, was to serve as a cacophonous reminder of city life until Boston mercifully sank it underground in the 1920s.

This location is in the finest residence section of the city and though but a short distance from street car facilities they are far enough removed to insure quiet and entire freedom from the usual traffic of a public thoroughfare.

Care of Sick   Special provision has been made for cases of sickness requiring isolation or more than ordinary care. For this purpose a hospital room has been constructed in each section and arranged with an anteroom containing double doors and equipped with special sanitary provisions to insure safety for those who are well and comfort for the sick.

Telephones and Bells   An electric bell communicates directly from the matron's room to all rooms in her section. Telephones are also provided on each floor. It is indeed difficult to imagine more complete buildings than these homes for the women students of the New England Conservatory of Music.

Cost   The cost of room and board ranges from $7.00 to $8.00 per week for double rooms (two persons in each room), and from $8.00 to $10.00 per week for single rooms. A few specially fitted rooms on the first floor may be secured at special rates. All bills are payable monthly in advance. Names will be received and choice of rooms allowed in order of application.

11

Three residential units, named after the school's first board presidents—Frost, Dana, Gardner—were constructed on Hemenway Street, adding to Chadwick's vision for a modern conservatory.

Plans must be filed and approved by this Department before
a permit for erection will be granted. *No.*

Application for Permit to Build.

(1st and 2d CLASS BUILDING *SEPTEMBER 13 1901.* 1901.

Boston, September, 9,

To the

BUILDING COMMISSIONER:

The undersigned hereby applies for a permit to build, according to the followi
specifications :—

1. Location, No. Huntington Ave. Gainsboro St. & St. Botolph St.
2. Nearest cross street? xxxxxxxxxxxx ....Ward
3. Name of Owner is New England Conservatory of Music Address Boston
4. " Builder is? Thompson-Starrett Company "183 Essex St. Boston.
5. " Architect is? Wheelwright & Haven "102 Boylston St. Boston.
6. Purpose of building is? Instruction in music. Stores? xxxxxxx
7. How many families? xxxxxxxxxxxx
8. How near the line of the street? 8 ft. Width of street? xxxxxx
9. Will the building be erected on solid or filled land? Filled. If in block, how many xxxxxx
10. Size of building, No. of feet front? 193' No. of feet rear, 193' No. of feet deep, 133'
    No. of stories in height, 3 ; No. of feet in height from sidewalk to highest point of roof. xxxx
11. Number of feet in
12. Number of feet in
13. Will foundation be
14. External walls, 1s
    Party walls, 1s
    Are the party walls
15. What will be the m
16. Will the roof be flat
17. What will be the ma
18. What will be means
19. Length of piles?
20. Number of rows?
21. Distance on centres
22. Diameter top?
23. How capped?
24. Piles cut off at what
25. Are there any hoistw
26. How is the building
27. Floors, how deafened? xxxxxxxxxxxx x
28. Fire stops to be provided? xxxxxxxxxxxxxxxx
29. Means of extinguishing fire? xxxxxxxxxxxxxxxxxxxxx
30. Size of floor beams? 7"8-9-10-12"15" Steel beams, Span? Varies Distance O. C.
31. " headers and trimmers? xxxxxxxxxxxxxxx "
32. " rafters? xxxxxxxxxxxxx
33. Stairways enclosed in brick walls? Yes,
34. Thickness of such walls? 12"
35. Stairway halls, how finished? Plastered, Estimated cost?

**If the building is to be occupied for a Tenement or Lodging House or Family Hotel, give
the following particulars:**

36. What is the height of cellar?
37. What will be the height of ceiling on first story, second, third, fourth,
    fifth, sixth, seventh, eighth,

That boom gave new strength to Boston's workers. Labor leaders campaigned for more pay, using strikes to strengthen their hand. Jordan and Chadwick were among their victims. They had planned to move out of Franklin Square in the summer of 1902, allowing plenty of time to prepare for a hectic fall. But a series of strikes in the construction industry put paid to their expectations. When registration day arrived on September 18, administrators dashed in just ahead of the students to find little more than a shell of the new building.

The NEC *Magazine* alluded to "somewhat unsettled conditions" on Huntington Avenue. In fact, the place was a mess. An electricians' strike meant unfinished walls, a confusion of wires, and no electricity. A threatened strike by piano and organ workers promised not only a dark but a silent Conservatory. At the core of this unfinished work sat the bare bones of a great hall. Chadwick announced that Jordan Hall at NEC would open in January, then energetically farmed out the school's concerts to other venues or pushed recitals back. Students played in the Music Hall, Tremont Temple, and even Sleeper Hall until the new building's recital hall, located beside Jordan, was dedicated on November 5. Henry Dunham's organ recital, scheduled as the Conservatory's inauguration on October 9, went off as planned, but at the Shawmut Congregational Church.

Chadwick tossed faculty recitals, orchestral rehearsals, and opera practices into the school's new recital hall. When Jordan Hall at NEC was finally finished in June, he rushed in the commencement exercises. On June 24, 1903, he and Board President Gardner welcomed thirty-six graduates onto the new stage and promised a real musical inauguration in the fall.

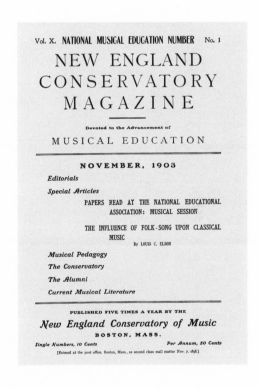

A sample New England Conservatory Magazine, *the school's monthly publication*

The ceremony went off without mishap, though the *Globe* warned that the new hall's precipitous stairs meant patrons "would be pretty sure to tumble and roll." Workers applied finishing touches to the building that summer, installing both a new organ and the towering statue of Beethoven. The organ, like so much else, had been donated by Eben Jordan, 2nd. It was, as Henry Dunham conceded, more than adequate compensation for the "pathetic" fate of the old Music Hall instrument it replaced. Built in 1863 and costing $60,000, that "great organ" had dominated the Music Hall for two decades before being given to the Conservatory. But the St. James had no place for this particularly elegant white elephant, so Tourjée hid it in a shed out back. Chadwick tumbled onto it, evicted a decade's worth of mice, then sold it off, preferring the more practical, electrically powered $50,000 version that Jordan agreed to buy. The new organ enlivened the hall for a generation, until Boston humidity and railroad soot silenced it forever. (Today its delicate, yet utterly useless, fluting provides only visual accompaniment to performances in Jordan Hall at NEC.)

Like the great organ, Beethoven had migrated from the old Music Hall but had a happier history. Originally cast in 1855, the statue had been Charles Perkins's gift to the Handel & Haydn Society. He had scoured Europe for the right sculptor, then commissioned Thomas Crawford, heartened by the fact that Crawford had designed the Indian atop the Capitol dome (which few people had ever seen), that he was Nathaniel Hawthorne's nephew, and that he belonged to Boston society. For six tons of bronze, the piece had traveled a great deal: Crawford sent it to Munich for a "suitable celebration" of Beethoven's death. From there, it went on to Boston, taking up residence in the Athenaeum for a year before settling in at the Music Hall. The Handel & Haydn Society "loaned" it to the Conservatory in 1902, before making it a permanent gift in 1951. Although he hadn't intended it, the statue became Perkins's most lasting gift to NEC.

On October 20, 1903, Conservatory guests filed in the Huntington entrance past Crawford's imposing Beethoven and gazed upon the new organ while they awaited the formal debut of Jordan Hall at NEC. NEC seized on the occasion not only to introduce the school's new facility but to advertise its new status under Chadwick. Major Higginson—"the 'King Ludwig' of Boston music"—came to give his blessing and to appeal to others to take up the burden that he, and now Jordan, had shouldered. In his moment of triumph, Chadwick stepped to the podium and conducted the BSO in his own *Melpomene*. Gericke followed with the *Eroica*.

But nothing was so obvious a success as the hall itself. Jordan, Chadwick, and Wheelwright had resisted the temptation to imitate Symphony Hall. Instead, they opted for the opposite effect. While Symphony Hall was deep and narrow, notable for its long aisles, recessed balconies, elaborate statuary, and high ceiling, Jordan Hall at NEC was a short, wide expanse with a raised central loge, smaller sloped aisles, stark adornment, and looming balcony. Its tilted floor seats and thrusting balcony pulled audiences forward in their seats, set the wide expanse of stage before each listener, and gave everyone, from the first-floor row to the last balcony seat, a chance to see.

And to hear. Thanks to Harvard physics professor Wallace C. Sabine, America's reigning acoustics wizard who had also assisted in making Symphony Hall the first scientifically designed auditorium, the sound of Jordan Hall at NEC shone clear, undiminished, and true. Not even the powerful organ could befuddle the more delicate notes of strings and reeds. Critics came away amazed, yet they had not heard the place at its best. For BSO musicians, used to the distances in their own hall, had played a little heavily; their sound had a trace of an echo. The smaller ensemble with less formidable musicians, such as the Conservatory orchestra, found it a friendly, forgiving place with a soft, full, rich sound.

Jordan Hall at NEC gave Chadwick a new opportunity, and he seized on it to transform his school into a modern conservatory. He concentrated on music and on talent. In keeping with America's growing concern about the quality of education, he worked to reorganize the Conservatory "on a university basis," hiring more professional faculty, and rationalizing and enlarging his curriculum. He also began to develop a diploma-granting institution, urging students to earn diplomas rather than drop by for lessons. He divested the peripheral schools that Tourjée had accrued. In 1900 he merged the Conservatory's School of Fine Arts with the Cowles Art School. In 1902 he sent his School of Elocution and Dramatic Action to Emerson College of Oratory. That new arrangement, he explained, meant lost tuition but ended "duplication of instruction." In 1906 he negotiated an arrangement with Harvard so that his students might choose from a wider selection of classes, and Harvard's musicians might study for more serious performance. And in 1910 he sold off the Conservatory's piano-tuning school to its chairman, Oliver Faust. The Faust School of Piano Tuning lasted several generations at 29 Gainsborough Street, until the Conservatory again needed to expand.

Chadwick improved the faculty. He imported Bimboni, brought back George Henschel to teach voice, and took on the new bride of Timothée Adamowski, Antoinette Szumowska-Adamowski, a considerable talent in her own right and the only female student Paderewski had ever condescended to train.

He also strengthened the school in his own field: musical theory. He kept Faelten's solfeggio classes but added orchestration as well as harmony and counterpoint—still the bases of the Conservatory's theory curriculum. And he hired good people to teach. In his first term, he brought in John Wallace Goodrich, who had studied with him and Dunham before making the obligatory trek to Munich for further training with Rheinberger. In 1900 he took on one of Goodrich's neighbors and childhood friends: Frederick Converse. Like Goodrich, Converse had studied with Chadwick and Rheinberger, and his hiring was something of a coup. Not only had his recent Symphony in D been debuted by Gericke and the BSO, but his prosperous dairy provided milk for NEC's dormitories at seven cents a quart. Arthur Shepherd, who had first come to the Conservatory at the age of twelve, returned to teach theory in 1909. Shepherd was another Chadwick student who, instead of going to Munich, had gone to Salt Lake City, where he had taught, organized, and conducted music. Perhaps because he had missed the exposure to Rheinberger, he was something of a modernist. His Violin Sonata showed the influence of the new wave of French composers, and his songs drew upon such contemporary poets as W.E. Henley, Walter de la Mare, and John Masefield.

Chadwick wanted his Conservatory to provide "a good general education." So he reduced the school's chaotic four terms to a more manageable two, then established formal junior and senior classes, with a regular curriculum leading to a diploma. He created a School of Literature and Expression and an art department. And he agreed to loan out his precious Jordan Hall stage for Shakespeare carnivals, dramatic productions, and performances of modern dance.

In January 1915 he invited Renée Longy to teach the "rhythmic gymnastics" she had studied under Jaques Dalcroze at the Institute for Eurhythmics in Switzerland. Sensible Americans regarded Dalcroze as a crank of the first order, and eurhythmics must have further hardened Chadwick's Yankee arteries. But he was willing to try anything to enhance his students' understanding of music, since he had a shrewd sense of how little they knew. "The average student," he complained, "usually guesses at the time-value of a group of notes or rests by the amount of ink they contain and when they are thirty-seconds and sixty-fourths, especially if any are dotted, he loses his head altogether."

His ambition was to educate creative musicians, to "get the student to hear through his eyes and see through his ears." If eurhythmic stomping about Jordan Hall at NEC helped, then he was prepared to tolerate a school of stomping, but better-trained, musicians. Chadwick welcomed any expedient. He downplayed the fierce rivalry among defenders of the English solfa, French solfeggio, and American public school systems of ear training. He cared little about the pedagogical clutter, so long as the students learned. In 1898 he imported kindergarten teachers to demonstrate the Fletcher Musical System, another in a long series of well-advertised attempts to teach music effortlessly. Convinced that students had to learn more about music and learn it younger, he was willing to look at his art "from the child's point of view," even when that meant tinkering with puzzles and toys. And in 1901 he turned his attention to improving musical pedagogy, hoping to find "the shortest road to solid musical achievement." But he typically warned students that he did not intend "to coddle [their] lazy bones."

Despite his efforts, Chadwick had no illusions that he had succeeded. In 1900 he admitted that NEC was "far from considering its students eligible" for the new bachelor of music diploma, since they still tended to enroll for occasional courses, rather than pursue degrees.

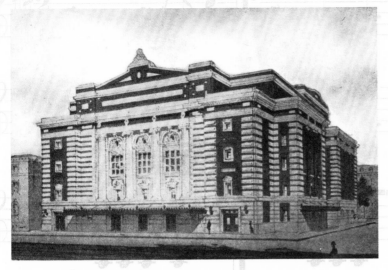

The Opera House—also donated by Jordan—and Symphony Hall joined Jordan Hall at NEC to form the musical backbone of the rapidly growing cultural district along Huntington Avenue.

Background: A score from The Musical Herald

New England Conservatory of Music, Boston, Mass.

The elegant and acoustically perfect Jordan Hall at NEC, and its original floor plans

Chadwick's greatest success, however, was in raising the Conservatory's musical standards without endangering its stability. Reviewing his finances, Chadwick confessed that he was "quite happy over the results." Thanks to his hard work, and Jordan's generosity, the Conservatory no longer labored under the weight of crushing debt. Jordan had donated $131,500 for the new building alone, including $50,000 for the organ and another $31,500 for land on Huntington Avenue—a parcel that would later be the site of Brown Hall. In 1913, Chadwick had the pleasure of announcing that an anonymous donor had given $100,000 to pay off pressing debts and to provide much-needed scholarships. Four years (and another $200,000) later, the community learned the name of its benefactor: Mrs. Robert Evans, reclusive wife of the president of the American Rubber Company. So shy that it pained her to see her own name, Evans aided the Conservatory's scholarship endowment drives. Only after her death did Boston awaken to the extent of her generosity: she had given almost $400,000 to the Conservatory. She and Jordan proved the school's financial saviors.

Their gifts enabled Chadwick to reduce NEC's staggering debt to a more manageable $75,000. For the first time in its history, the school could afford to look ahead to its needs, rather than back at its debts. So Chadwick promptly plunged into the Conservatory's first systematic fund-raising efforts: the 1913 scholarship and the 1917 endowment drives. He was determined to train the most promising young musicians, rather than those best able to pay tuition. Chadwick recognized the Conservatory's need for more scholarships. During the school's hungry days, his predecessors had looked upon scholarships with suspicion, but Chadwick focused on talent. He understood that the modern conservatory needed scholarship money to attract and sustain promising young musicians. Antonín Dvořák said as much. He had utterly relied on scholarships and awards for his own education, and the memory of that stayed with him all his life. *In Music in America,* he had insisted that "art...does not 'pay,' to use an American expression—

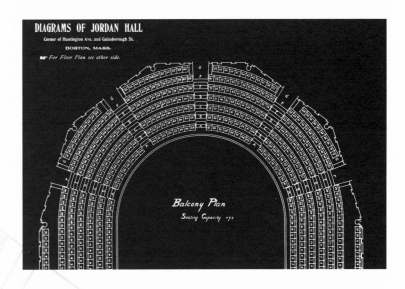

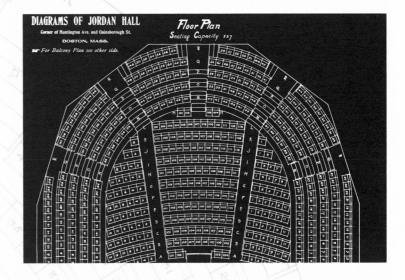

Sample of the Conservatory's yearbook,
The Neume.

Sinfonia Club, 1920

at least not in the beginning—and…the art that has to pay its own way is apt to become vitiated and cheap."

Chadwick shared both Dvořák's hopes and fears that music on the cheap was likely to be nasty. He too had known lean years. His memories of Munich included not only lessons with Rheinberger but days of going without food to pay for them. So he was not about to trust musical Darwinism to provide either good students or good music. Instead he energetically pursued money for scholarships. He began by campaigning for the Beneficent Society, an odd assortment of Bostonian grande dames, Conservatory alumnae, and good-hearted employees who offered modest sums to needy students. Founded in 1886 and first led by Julia Ward Howe, the society raised $17,000 in twenty-five years, doling out as little as $10 at a time to 224 different students.

Then Chadwick approached Boston society, a world he knew to his Yankee fingertips. He appealed to his trustees first, and they dipped into their pockets. In 1910, Chadwick launched the Tourjée Memorial Student Aid Fund, hoping to raise $10,000 by the 1911 commencement, then earmarked a quarter of Evans's first gift for still more scholarships. He also convinced her to provide five Evans scholarships for two students in piano, two in voice, and one in violin or cello. His 1917 endowment drive targeted another $150,000 for student aid: a third to the Tourjée fund, the remainder to provide twenty scholarships for needy musicians.

While he had no great love for dormitories, Chadwick nevertheless understood his responsibilities to the students who lived in them. During his tenure, residential students made the Conservatory into a community as well as a place for music. In 1907 they sported their way through an "enthusiastic tennis wave" that crested with a Denée Cup competition—the first in a long history of genial athletic matches. In 1910 they demonstrated their fondness for the joke by awarding themselves letters in "feetball"—parodying the mania for spectator sport sweeping America's universities. And in 1911 they indulged in the short-lived fad of "aesthetic walking," which amounted to strolling around the Fens.

Conservatory activities, though, were not taken up entirely by music, practice, and sport. In 1908 students organized the first Costume Carnival at Symphony Hall. For a generation, they donned outlandish dress and headed down Huntington Avenue, where they waged something like a dance, promenade, and burlesque all rolled into one. They also kept up the tradition of Founder's Day, leading an annual descent on Nantasket's roller coasters, carousels, and "bump the bumps."

On a slightly more serious note, they formed the school's first Greek letter societies. Faelten had authorized the first sorority—Alpha Chi Omega—in 1896; the Sinfonia Club for men appeared in 1898 (to be reformed as the Alpha Chapter of Phi Mu Alpha Sinfonia in 1901), followed by the Mu Phi Epsilon sorority (1903), the Pan-Hellenic Society (1910), the Kappa Gamma Psi fraternity (1913), and Sigma Alpha Iota (1915).

Since the school continued to attract far more women than men, the role of women remained a prominent topic of discussion on Huntington Avenue. As the suffragette movement caught public attention, first in Great Britain and then at home, Conservatory women took up "the Cause." In 1896 they stormed through a combination mock election and demonstration for the vote. Their boisterous meeting echoed the national sentiment: they cheered themselves hoarse for William Jennings Bryan, then voted for William McKinley. Four years later, they repeated the demonstration, but in the wake of the Spanish American War, the cheers, as well as the votes, went to McKinley.

The Sigma Alpha Iota sorority, 1925

But their concern for women's issues lasted well into peacetime. Students seized every occasion to discuss women's rights. In dorm meetings, recitals, convocations, and chapel services, they argued for those rights. In 1899, Nellie Van Ness took up the matter at graduation, leading a perplexed crowd of parents through the issue of "Woman and Her Possibilities," concluding with a passionate appeal for women's suffrage.

That kind of enthusiasm flooded into more practical matters as well. While the men cavorted through "feetball," women in the dorms debated a new, fashionable issue: "Harem skirts, shall we wear them?" For women burdened with ten to fifteen pounds of wool, cotton, ivory buttons, iron hoops, and whalebone corset stays, dress was more than a matter of taste. Amelia Bloomer's loose tunic and pantaloons had given way to the trousers and petticoats of the Rational Dress Society, and Conservatory students gave harem pants an overwhelming vote of approval—though the men unanimously plumped for skirts, and the women agreed that they were unwilling to wear the pants anyway.

Their enthusiasm for women's issues crested with Nordica's return to her alma mater in 1909. Although in her decline, she looked back on a career that had taken her from two-dollar voice lessons with O'Neill in the old Music Hall to private tutoring with the equally formidable Cosima Wagner. She had sung in the opera houses of St. Petersburg, London, Paris, New York, and Bayreuth and had entertained such diverse symbols of a passing age as Tsar Alexander II, King Edward VII, and Buffalo Bill. Her extraordinary range and gift

for languages had made her one of the most successful Wagnerian heroines of her time, while her renderings of *Home, Sweet Home; Nearer My God to Thee;* and *Rosalie* had made her rich. But three unhappy and expensive marriages had also taught her about the precarious rights of women. At the Chicago World's Fair, she met Susan B. Anthony. In England, she followed the protests of Emmeline Pankhurst's Women's Social and Political Union. She became a powerful voice for women's rights, and also a good-humored one. During the campaign for women's suffrage in California, men told her that poll booths were too rough-and-tumble for the weaker sex. In that case, she replied, "they should be brought up to the level of our trolley cars."

She was a formidable woman, whether dressed in the peasant garb of Marguerite or armed with Brunhilde's spear. And when she visited NEC, she spoke, as well as sang, from the heart. She reminded students of the difficulties facing women, urged them to support "the Cause," and then, without missing a beat, sang from Jordan Hall at NEC's stage. A legend come home, she inspired a new generation of Conservatory women.

In the first decade of the twentieth century, Conservatory women—like those in higher education all across America—found new, but still limited, opportunities. NEC singers, including not only Nordica but Louisa Homer (who sang with the Metropolitan Opera Company from 1900 to 1929) and Maude Reese Davies (soloist for the new John Philip Sousa Band), attested to the prospects of success and reminded students that, only a few years earlier, each had been "one of them." Composers like Amy Beach and Mabel Wheeler Daniels (who directed the Radcliffe Glee Club and Simmons College music department) showed that women were no longer confined to the "receptive" end of genius. But there was also the example of Virginia Stickney, who had taken her degree from the Conservatory, driven herself until she was recognized as a cellist of exceptional talent and artistry, perhaps the outstanding talent in America, only to spend her best years eking out a living from occasional engagements and odd teaching jobs.

Symphony orchestras all across America competed for the finest musicians available, yet women like Stickney could not even apply. For them, there was only one opportunity: the Women's Orchestra of Los Angeles, founded by Hadley Hamilton in 1892, then turned over to Cora Calvert Foy, the first woman to direct an orchestra in America. For more than thirty years, that remained the only chance for an American woman to play in a professional orchestra, no matter how talented she was. Leopold Stokowski, conducting the Pittsburgh orchestra, campaigned against what he saw not only as an injustice but an "incomprehensible blunder." "We are," he protested, "sacrificing accomplishment to tradition."

Chadwick, too, lamented that tradition. He gloried in the fact that in 1910–11 alone, his Conservatory placed fifteen graduates in America's leading orchestras. But he apologized for the fact that they were all men. "It is not impossible," he said by way of comfort, "that in the future women will find themselves playing in symphony orchestras." But he accepted the laws of his musical world and did not welcome women into his own orchestra until the Great War. Only then, when thinning ranks threatened two decades of work, did he accept women into his orchestra. Once he did, though, he had the good sense to keep them.

Chadwick always kept his Conservatory open to visiting musical stars. While still in Franklin Square, he had welcomed Louisa Homer and her composer husband, Sidney—yet another of his former students who had worked with Rheinberger. He also greeted Fritz Kreisler, making his first American tour, and squeezed Victor Herbert and his Pittsburgh Orchestra onto the tiny Sleeper stage in October 1900. Herbert, who had taken over Patrick Gilmore's band in 1892, was making the transition from popular to classical music. Chadwick, with a strong distaste for the "dishonest, inartistic, and miserable stuff" that Herbert was forsaking, gave the young conductor his blessing.

The move to Huntington Avenue gave Chadwick a stage better suited to his ambitions. For the next fifteen years, he populated it with some of Boston's—and the world's—most impressive musicians. Only eighteen days after the hall's inauguration, Jacques Thibaud played for Conservatory students. In the next decade, Jordan Hall at NEC welcomed back the now famous Fritz Kreisler; saluted Ferruccio Busoni, who had once taught piano at NEC; and hailed the aging Vladimir de Pachmann, whose days as a pianist rivaling Rubinstein and Paderewski were drawing to a close. Among the voices heard on that stage were the promising, as all agreed Edith Mason's was, and the mature, as old neighbors preferred to think of Nordica's.

But Jordan Hall at NEC was not simply a display case for celebrities. It was a theater for music. In its first fifteen years, new music flowed from its stage. On January 31, 1906, Jordan Hall at NEC hosted its first opera: the world premiere of Frederick Converse's *Pipe of Desire.* Wallace Goodrich spent so much time recruiting musicians, resurrecting a Conservatory chorus, and preparing the hall for its debut that Converse (who had given up tending cows in favor of educating Harvard students) worried about his friend's "overflowing and perhaps injudicious enthusiasm." But Goodrich was right: *The Pipe* was a breakthrough for the Conservatory and for American opera. Jordan Hall at NEC carried off its premiere with style and grace. Its large stage, clean sound, and outstanding sight lines offered an excellent environment for nurturing new works.

In that case, Converse's opera was little more than a reworking of the aeolian harp and Orpheus legends, with some exciting music and a great deal of pointless cavorting. Philip Hale, the tendentious critic for the old *Boston Transcript,* damned its weak plot and uninspired motivation. Converse, he insisted, had not made his characters matter. But he recognized that the music had great promise, and he was right: *The Pipe* moved on to become the first American opera produced by the Metropolitan Opera Company. That marked not only Converse's growth as a composer of note but the emergence of a new generation of American music, drawing upon national melodies, though not yet national themes.

Andrew Carnegie once said his fond ambition for a prized steel mill was to wear it out as quickly as possible. Chadwick seemed to feel the same way about Jordan Hall at NEC, particularly for new music and Boston's tradition of outstanding amateur performances. In the *Transcript,* Hale sniffed that Jordan Hall at NEC concerts had merely a "semi-private character." But to the community, they offered the opportunity to hear some of the most promising modern performances in music. In 1906, hard on the heels of Converse's *Pipe,* Goodrich led the NEC Orchestra through the first Boston performance of César Franck's *Psyché.* To make his interest in modern music clear, he concluded the program with Gluck's *Iphigenia.* In January 1907, Goodrich debuted another of Converse's works in Jordan Hall at NEC, introducing the orchestral version of *Jeanne d'Arc.* The piece so impressed Dr. Karl Muck, newly appointed conductor of the Boston Symphony, that he added it to his March program for New York. And in February 1908, Converse again returned to Jordan Hall at NEC, where his *Job* made its Boston debut, with Goodrich again conducting a joint performance by BSO musicians and the NEC chorus. Goodrich— who seemed to make a career of introducing his friends' music—also premiered Converse's *Sacrifice* in January 1911. Jordan Hall at NEC, which had earlier stood in for mythological Greece and the Holy Land, now took on the air of Spanish California, as Converse at last developed a compelling American theme: the moral complexities behind Manifest Destiny. Critics praised the improvements of music and materials in his second opera but agreed that he "should not be in haste to compose his third."

Converse took their criticisms to heart. "Perhaps they are right," he wrote to one friend. "Who knows?" His one-time teacher did. Chadwick dismissed such reviewers as "newspaper reptiles" and continued his own composing. During his busy days as Conservatory director, he managed to complete some of his most ambitious works. His *Euterpe,* debuted by the BSO in 1903, introduced American syncopations to the orchestra and its audiences. His *Suite Symphonic* featured not only a clever parody of Debussy but also, in the middle of its solemn intermezzo, a cakewalk. His *Tam O'Shanter* again presented classical music with a twist, incorporating Scottish airs and Burns's poetry into a warm, simple melody. But his most ambitious work, and his greatest failure, was his opera *The Padrone.* A brutal look at the fate of Italian immigrants, it provided a contrast to Puccini's enormously popular *Girl of the Golden West.* But Padrone was too "humble …and too true to life," though it remains, to this day, one of the most discussed works in the large repertoire of unproduced music.

Educated in Rheinberger's fierce German classicism, Chadwick nevertheless nursed a tenderness for contemporary English music. In that, he shared his audience's Anglophilia: the only anthem that ever induced Boston socialites to rise was *God Save the King.* So Jordan Hall at NEC became the stage for idyllic Albion. In 1915, for example, Chadwick led his musicians through the American debut of Sir Charles Villiers Stanford's Seventh Symphony. Now almost forgotten, Stanford was then at the peak of a typically English musical career: his aristocratic family and early promise had been so richly rewarded that his titles—professor of music at the Royal College, conductor of the London Bach Choir, professor of music at Cambridge, conductor of the Leeds Festival, and knight of the realm—shone more impressively than his work ever did. A friend to von Bülow, Saint-Saëns, and Brahms, he was a terror to his students, including Vaughan Williams and Gustav Holst, both of whom smarted— even as adults—when he called their music sloppy, dubious, and vulgar. He was a kind of English Chadwick, and his music appealed to both the conductor and the pedagogue in his American counterpart.

In November 1917, Chadwick handed the baton over to Percy Grainger, who led the NEC orchestra through songs and selections from his works. Although born in Australia and of minor talent, Grainger's cultural submission to things English transformed him into an Englishman right out of vaudeville. He constituted a one-man mission for English song, and his enthusiasm compensated for thoroughly familiar music. But those songs enthralled a generation of Anglophiles who were not yet prepared for show tunes or jazz.

Chadwick, however, was too ambitious to litter his new stage with too many celebrities and old tunes. During that era, he championed new American music, especially that written by his own students and disciples. In December 1914 he led his seventy musicians through a program featuring two new cantatas: Henry Hadley's *Golden Prince* and Arthur Foote's *Gateway of Isphael.* Hadley had first come to his attention by winning the Jordan Prize for symphonic composition in 1901; Foote was yet another NEC alumnus and Harvard man—as well as the first American to receive a master of music degree. And in 1918, Chadwick handed over his baton to Arthur Shepherd, who then conducted the world premiere of his *Fantasie Humoresque.* Shepherd had studied with Chadwick, won the Paderewski Prize in 1901, and taught harmony at NEC since 1909. What made the moment especially poignant was that the thirty-eight-year-old composer had just returned from France: his last job had been conducting an army band under artillery fire in the trenches at Verdun.

EDMUND WHEELWRIGHT: BOSTON'S FIRST CITY ARCHITECT

The whimsical Harvard Lampoon building in Cambridge

The ornate Horticultural Hall

From the grandiose Baroque Horticultural Hall to its more sedate neighbor nearby, Jordan Hall at New England Conservatory, Boston's distinctive architecture owes much to Edmund Wheelwright. As the first city architect from 1891 to 1895, he designed not only Horticultural Hall and Jordan Hall, with his firm Wheelwright and Haven, but many more buildings: the Boston Opera House, which was demolished in 1958; the Longfellow Bridge; the Charles E. Perkins Elementary School (now the Pine Street Inn); Lampoon Castle in Cambridge, which houses Harvard's undergraduate humor magazine; the Massachusetts Historical Society; and the Park Street subway's original granite and bronze entrances. He also had a hand with Symphony Hall, as chief architect with McKim, Mead, & White.

Boston architecture is also indebted to Eben Jordan, 2nd. In addition to financing Wheelwright's Jordan Hall at NEC and the Boston Opera House, he also contributed to the Emerson Majestic Theatre. An interesting note: Wheelwright designed Jordan's summer mansion in Manchester-by-the-Sea.

The Boston Opera House, demolished in 1958

GEORGE WHITEFIELD CHADWICK: AN AMERICAN SCHOOL

6

The coming of the Great War took America, and the musical world, by surprise. Many of the Conservatory faculty were in Europe during the harrowing days of August 1914. Their escape brought a sense of the conflict back to Huntington Avenue. Clement Lenom, oboist and solfège teacher, first heard rumors of war while in Bayreuth. He rushed back to his native Belgium, only to find that the Germans had already taken over. Everywhere he went he found "devastation and the wake of fighting—houses down, whole villages down, crops gone, nothing but ruin." It was the first campaign of the war. For four more years, the world watched as the devastation spread.

August 1914 also found Henry Dunham touring Europe on holiday. He settled in Switzerland, enjoying a cool respite from the warmest, driest summer in memory. When war came, he fled to Rome, hoping to find passage home. Instead,

he stumbled into fear and confusion. As the Italian government equivocated, Americans rushed for the ports, only to find themselves stranded, their money draining away. Banks refused American checks. Wealthy tourists found themselves trapped and penniless. Dunham escaped that fate: he had invested in the new American Express travelers' checks, and Italian banks readily accepted them.

But his only way out was to sail for England, through waters patrolled by German submarines. After an anxious, but uneventful, voyage, he made for Scotland, where he thrust himself upon the hospitality of Eben Jordan, summering at the old Inverary Castle. Finally, he found a ship headed for home, though it was so crowded that he had to sleep—or spend long nights playing cards—on deck.

By the time Lenom and Dunham returned to Boston, America had settled in for the duration, "too proud to fight." Artists of every nation flocked to or remained here. It was an indication of the age's innocence that Boston society expected BSO musicians to enlist, though "investigation proved to the contrary." Local music profited from their decision: Paderewski, Kreisler, Madame Melba, and Farrar all performed with the BSO during the first year of the war. As David Bispham, America's leading Wagnerian baritone, pointed out, the war was a kind of windfall for America: "No commercial or professional enterprise," he told *Opera Magazine*, "will respond so quickly to the present European conflict as the musical life of this country." The same parochialism swept through the Conservatory: its first discussion of the war was headlined "Boston's Greatest Concert Opportunity."

Even in its opening days, however, there were a few who better understood the obligations, as well as the opportunities, of war. Paderewski, who had used his celebrity to speak up for the Polish people, now threw himself—and his concert earnings—into the cause. In 1915 he established the Polish Victims' Relief Fund, then began a grueling American tour to raise money and agitate for a free Poland. He was joined by Madame Szumowska-Adamowski,

The entire country was caught up in World War I patriotism. Here, a farewell parade for the 26th division treks down Boylston Street.

who still taught piano at the Conservatory
and presided over the Friends of Poland,
raising more than $500,000 for orphans'
relief. Their efforts helped create
an independent Poland. Paderewski went on
to become his country's first prime
minister and sign the Treaty of Versailles.

But for most of Boston's musical
community, it was business as usual. There
were hard words about Karl Muck being
a Hessian, but he led the BSO through its
spectacularly successful 1915–16 season
with little controversy. The Metropolitan
Opera Company organized a Wagner
festival for the summer of 1915, staging it
in Harvard's massive football stadium.
And the NEC Orchestra kept Jordan Hall at
NEC filled, as Chadwick introduced new
composers to smaller, but more comfortable, audiences. For the moment, it seemed
that America was to escape not only the
war but its propaganda of atrocity and
reprisal. As late as December 1914, the
Conservatory's *Magazine* protested against
the belligerent nationalism and hatred
orchestrated by both sides. It focused its
anger on the upcoming scourge of
America, the "lascivious" Bunny Hop.

The moment was not to last.
Woodrow Wilson had warned that if
Americans went to war, "they will forget
there ever was such a thing as tolerance…
conformity will be the only virtue."
When he declared war in April 1917, a frantic
nation acted out his fears. Constitutional
liberties were sacrificed for hopes of victory
in Europe and "100 percent Americanism"
at home. Those who stood up for their

rights, and those who blundered into their
way, were run over. Under the weight of
relentless propaganda—called "war information"—people grew more and more
intolerant. German culture, from which the
country had drawn its ideals of music,
higher education, and lager beer, was now
denounced as Boche barbarism. Musical
zealots rushed to lead the stampede. In
New York, Fritz Kreisler was shouted down
by concertgoers. The Chicago Opera
Company responded by banning all German
works from its repertoire. Beethoven and
Bach were orthodox enough to escape
all that ban; genius made them honorary
Americans. But Wagner, Strauss, and
even Rheinberger were now denounced
unrepentant Huns.

The most ludicrous and terrifying
incident, however, struck at the heart of
the BSO. Scheduled to tour the East Coast,
the orchestra opened in Rhode Island
on October 30, 1917, and the *Providence
Journal* demanded that the audience "put
Professor Muck to the test." If he agreed to
play the "Star-Spangled Banner," he was
an American conductor; if he refused, he

was a Hun. That night, Muck conducted the program as scheduled, took his bow, left the stage, and so made the mistake of his life. The press denounced him as an enemy to the nation and bayed for his blood. Politicians rushed to give it to them. The *Journal* demanded that right-thinking Americans prevent Muck from ever performing again. In Baltimore, the orchestra's next stop, the mayor and police commissioner ordered its concert canceled and the conductor banned from the stage. In Washington, officials hinted at a spy network within the BSO.

Too late, Muck realized the awful implications of what he had not done. He apologized and explained. He tried to atone, but every act only confirmed the vigilantes' suspicions. First, he announced that neither he nor the orchestra had known the anthem well enough to do it justice, which further roused the indignation of the zealots. Then he agreed to play it

Recruitment efforts such as this one on Boston Common in 1917 convinced many American citizens to enlist. NEC students were not immune: many signed up at the encouragement of the Conservatory, whose officials saw the war as "a vacation on good pay."

at every performance. Patriots muttered that he did so with his back to the audience. He produced a letter from the Swiss legation revealing that he was not, in fact, a German at all, news that even friendly papers greeted with the headline "Dr. Muck Not an Enemy Alien." He also published a catalog of the orchestra's citizenship, which showed that only twenty-two of his musicians were German, while fifty-one were American. But critics pointed out that only seventeen of those Americans had been born here. The requirements for loyalty were growing too fast for poor Muck to keep up. He offered to resign; Higginson refused. The final humiliation came in March 1918, when Muck, who had led America's finest orchestra for eight years, was arrested and charged as an undesirable alien. Despite its debt to German music, its commitment to international culture, and its prominent statue of Beethoven, NEC bayed with the rest of the mob. At the height of the BSO fiasco, its *Magazine* warned that "we are not going to allow any traitorous highbrows to set their own standards of freedom by which to convert freedom into treason."

The war, though, evoked courage as well as hatred. And Conservatory students did their part. By the time of the armistice, 118 NEC men had enlisted, 40 had served in combat, and in the Argonne Forest fighting, one student—Frank Mills—had been badly gassed and another—Ludwig Staatler—killed. Conservatory women also made sacrifices for the cause. Elizabeth Wood, a 1913 graduate who had sung with the Boston Opera Company, toured the front, singing for the troops. She was later joined by Iva Ryder, a full-blooded Cherokee, who quit school, spent six months entertaining American soldiers along the front, and then, as soon as the armistice had been signed, returned to Huntington Avenue to complete her training.

The students' work was eagerly applauded by the school officials, who twice voted to encourage enlistment, though they had no idea what that meant. As late as October 1917, they urged their students to join the cause "singing and laughing, for they start an experience that will show its beneficial results through all their lives." Utterly ignorant of the realities of trench war, they likened army life to "a vacation on good pay."

That, of course, was the kind of stuff that English poet Wilfred Owen was even then savaging as "the old lie." But the Conservatory, as well as its students, prepared for its idea of war. When General Pershing announced that the army needed "stirring music," NEC teachers flocked to Washington and convinced the War Department to raise more bands and to commission band leaders. Wallace Goodrich organized a Red Cross auxiliary within school walls, and students supported the war by making bandages or collecting books and magazines.

Jordan Hall at NEC provided the focus for their war effort. In December 1916, at the height of Germany's undeclared submarine war on America, the drama school staged Emile Cammaerts's *Une Voix dans le Desert*, with music by Sir Edward Elgar. Despite its title, that song-play provided a gory, but patriotic, account of French heroism in the trenches. After April 1917, when the United States entered the war, the hall became a national resource, diverted to winning the war. In April 1918, Jesse Wilson Sayre, President Wilson's daughter, appeared there under the auspices of the YWCA. Later that month, students held a Liberty Bond mass meeting there. And in June, the Red Cross put it to better use, staging a concert by 140 violinists and inviting music lovers to donate ten cents for admission. As an additional curiosity, the Red Cross announced that a Puerto Rican child prodigy would play accompaniment: the fourteen-year-old Jesús Sanromá. Thus began a career that spanned another six decades and included many more money-raising efforts for his school.

The Conservatory did its part. Arthur Shepherd, old enough to sit out the war, resigned his teaching post and became a conductor for one of General Pershing's bands. He later treated his year in Europe as a kind of comic adventure, telling students that the worst of trench life was not the stench, or the rats, or the artillery fire, but the rain—since that washed the reeds right out of his saxophones.

On November 11, 1918, the Conservatory joined a weary world in laying aside the paraphernalia of war. The Red Cross Auxiliary disbanded, rationing came to an end, and tired veterans returned to their music. But the war had wrought profound changes in the Conservatory. Until August 1914 its repertoire had been German, focused on the age from Bach's sacred music to Brahms. Even American composers—including Chadwick—had been the heirs of that tradition, upholding the severe classicism of Rheinberger.

Now new music trickled out of Europe as austere modernists created a new language they called atonality. Composers like Schoenberg, Berg, Webern, and Stravinsky found few friends at the Conservatory. Even the more harmonious sounds of French impressionists like Debussy and Ravel met with opposition from the pedagogues. Just as they had resolutely ignored Brahms and Wagner in the closing years of the nineteenth century, Boston musical experts now shunned Schoenberg and Stravinsky. And in New Orleans, a young performer named Louis Armstrong was staking a claim to American music that few classicists were willing to consider.

Technical advances were simultaneously changing the face of music. Radio made music, and musical concerts, a part of the nation's growing leisure time, while primitive recordings gave a glimpse of what was to come.

As Henry Adams had earlier complained, "Genius dawned slowly on the Boston mind." Before the anti-Muck hysteria set in, the BSO had celebrated its successful 1915–16 season with thirty-nine German works, along with eleven French, eight Russian, fourteen other European, and nine American selections. The Conservatory dutifully followed the example set just down the street. Under Chadwick, the school's orchestra that year had played twenty-one German, fifteen French, five Russian, eight other European, and eight American works. But by 1918, both orchestras had made the move away from German classicism. Under Muck's successor, Henri Rabaud, the BSO played only twenty-eight German works, along with fifty-four French, nine Russian, seven other European, and nine American pieces. And Chadwick now offered only eleven of the German selections he so dearly loved. In their place, he conducted sixteen French, one Russian, nine other European, and three American compositions.

The BSO was in the throes of change. Henry Higginson died on November 14, 1919, bringing an end to his autocratic genius and to his loyal support for the Conservatory. As he confessed to Isabella Stewart Gardner, he had devoted his life to "beauty and duty"; his last act had been to entrust his great work to the care of a Board of Trustees. They turned resolutely away from the music Higginson had loved. In rapid succession they chose musical directors from the newer, less German schools. Henri Rabaud and Pierre Monteux, directors from 1918 until 1924, had been operatic conductors, trained in the new French music. Their successor, Serge Koussevitzky, introduced a new scope and repertoire to the orchestra, transforming the BSO from a museum of music into an orchestra on the edge of musical development. Koussevitzky made his ambitions clear: his debut concert featured Stravinsky.

A new order led the BSO. Boston, American, and even world premieres dotted every program. Music by Hindemith, Stravinsky, Webern, Schoenberg, and Bartók succeeded the ritual performances of German classicism. Before long, Conservatory students learned that, simply by walking down the street, they could hear the new music, whether it was the quiet beauty of Debussy's *La Mer* or the rattling energy of Bartók's Piano Concerto, played by the composer himself. They learned still more from Koussevitzky. Like his predecessors, he was "keenly alive to the importance of adequate preparation." His musicians found in their new conductor the talents of a "drill master," who concentrated on both "the aesthetic fundamentals" and the "little details of instrumental musicianship."

Although not so dramatically as the BSO, the NEC Orchestra also began to change. The German masters remained, but French music now appeared often, so regularly that the French government awarded the conductor, Wallace Goodrich, the Chevalier of the Legion of Honor for services to French music. New American music found a place in Jordan Hall at NEC as well. In 1928–29, for example, Goodrich conducted only twenty German compositions, along with eleven French and twenty-two American. Many of those were works by Chadwick and Frederick Converse.

BSO director Serge Koussevitzky put the Symphony on the edge of musical development with performances featuring Stravinsky and Schoenberg. The NEC Orchestra mirrored that trend, albeit more slowly.

Converse, though a traditional composer, produced some of the most interesting American music of the 1920s. As head of the Theory Department and later dean, he was intrigued by the possibilities of writing music for what he called the "photo-music drama": motion pictures. Eager for a new venture, he agreed to score the film *Puritan Passions*, a saga of the Salem witch trials, loosely based on Nathaniel Hawthorne's *Feathertop* and starring Mary Astor. Converse saw the movies as a distinctly American art, a mutual communion between sight and sound. So he provided descriptive music that gave a powerful emotional undercurrent to the drama and, at the same time, seized on the film's pictures to illustrate the subtleties of his music.

In scoring *Puritan Passions*, Converse became one of America's first serious composers to see the rich potential of this new form. He dreamed that "moving pictures of the land may play the role of the small opera houses of Europe," helping to create greater audiences for good music. On December 18, 1923, he listened as the NEC Orchestra played his score, with Goodrich conducting. The *Boston Evening Transcript* had dismissed the film as "a hodge-podge of semi-reality and specious symbolism," but it admired Converse's music and urged him to continue this work.

For the next decade, the NEC Orchestra plunged into a new repertoire. On November 16, 1923, students performed Stuart Mason's *Rhapsody on a Persian Air*, along with the more conventional Beethoven's Fifth Symphony. On February 22, 1925, they played Henry Hadley's tone poem, *Mr. Hadley's Ocean*, with the composer conducting, and followed that with his *Overture in Bohemia*. On December 18, 1925, the orchestra joined NEC's chorus to stage the first complete performance of local composer

By the late 1920s, the NEC Orchestra was a force in the Americanization of the nation's leading orchestras, with performances featuring works by George Chadwick and Frederick Converse.

Horatio Parker's *A.D. 1919*, written to honor the 8,000 Yale men who fought—and the 225 who died—in the Great War. And on November 19, 1925, the orchestra honored one of its own: Goodrich debuted two works by Seigi Abe, a Conservatory student whose *Tasogare* and *Kogawa no Hotori* echoed the fishermen's songs of his native Hokkaido.

By the end of the twenties, the NEC Orchestra had distinguished itself in three prominent ways: its musicianship rivaled that of most professional orchestras, it championed new American music, and it was becoming a force in the Americanization of the nation's leading orchestras.

Chadwick handed his baton to Goodrich in 1919, and the orchestra continued to thrive. "How many people in Boston have any idea of the quality of the student orchestra of the New England Conservatory of Music?" A.H.M., the music critic for the *Transcript*, asked. He tried to show them. Reviewing a single concert in November 1922, he pointed out that the orchestra offered music ranging from Chadwick's own *Elegy* to the Boston premiere of Ralph Vaughan Williams's *Pastoral Symphony*.

For that ensemble, as the *Evening Transcript* pointed out, "The rule is youth." Although a few BSO players still made their appearances as guest artists, the NEC Orchestra now stood on its own. As Boston's leading music critic argued, "The Conservatory band produces a tone that many a professional organization might envy." And it played American music. Koussevitzky, the acknowledged champion of new music, insisted that "the next Beethoven vill from Colorado come."

Chadwick and Goodrich expected to educate that great hope, but they were also determined to preserve the repertoire. While still conducting, Chadwick had regularly programmed his own works and those of his peers: Arthur Shepherd, Edward Ballantine, and Edward Burlingame Hill. Only later did American modernists like Copland, Gershwin, and Virgil Thomson come to be heard in Jordan Hall at NEC.

With the orchestra now in Goodrich's hands, Chadwick turned to other aspects of Conservatory life. In 1924 he ended its affiliation with Harvard and applied to the Massachusetts Legislature for authority to confer baccalaureate degrees. Permission was granted in 1925, and two years later Chadwick personally awarded the Conservatory's first bachelor of music to Ruth Elizabeth Austen—a former Radcliffe student who had won honors for her thesis, "A Genealogy of Nineteenth Century Violinists."

The Conservatory's baccalaureate program was rigorous and restricted. A decade after winning the right to confer the bachelor of music, Chadwick awarded only twenty-nine to a student body that numbered more than two thousand. He was determined to made his Conservatory a serious collegiate institution. He not only ended its affiliations and modernized its curriculum, but also introduced a new, and more demanding, Collegiate Department, which offered courses in English literature, psychology, and the fine arts. His reforms increased the school's professionalism and attracted stronger students. It reduced its dependence on the meaningless diploma. Chadwick made sure of that. "Degrees with us," he reminded his students, "are something more than epithets, and anyone who received them is pretty sure to have earned them."

Chadwick envisioned the Conservatory as "a university of the musical arts" that would be part of the Fenway's "great composite university." In 1902, most of the land west of the Conservatory had been nothing more than an "uncouth salt marsh inherited from colonial days" and an undersized ballpark for the Boston Braves. By the 1920s, the area had blossomed into Boston's center for the arts and education: the Museum of Fine Arts, YMCA, Isabella Stewart Gardner Museum, and Boston Opera House joined Northeastern College, Wentworth Institute, Simmons College, Boy's Latin, Notre Dame Academy, two arts schools, two medical schools, a dental school, and a school for nurses in making the old Fens into Boston's great cultural center. By 1930, as Chadwick pointed out, "nowhere else in America is there such a concourse of young people studying various arts and sciences as may be found on and near Fenway."

Wallace Goodrich, conductor of the NEC Orchestra, took Chadwick's place as director in 1931.

George Brown, chairman of the Board
of Trustees, financed the Conservatory's new
recital hall.

*Brown Hall was not only physically
attractive, with its warm wood, adorned
ceiling, and gleaming fixtures,
but functional, serving as the Conservatory's
auditorium, lecture hall, and ballroom.*

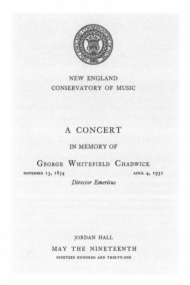

NEW ENGLAND
CONSERVATORY OF MUSIC

A CONCERT

IN MEMORY OF

GEORGE WHITEFIELD CHADWICK

NOVEMBER 13, 1854   APRIL 4, 1931

Director Emeritus

JORDAN HALL

MAY THE NINETEENTH

NINETEEN HUNDRED AND THIRTY-ONE

*The program for Chadwick's memorial
concert in 1931*

His Conservatory was a prominent
part of the Fenway's new life. After the
war, enrollment had swollen to more than
three thousand students, arriving from
forty-six states and twenty-two foreign
lands. Chadwick gloried in that. He recognized that "under a New England name
a genuinely national conservatory of music
has been built up in Boston in the past
fifty-three years." Now, he pressed for expansion. Enrollments continued to climb.
His school needed more space and another
hall. So he seized on the land Eben Jordan,
2nd, had provided in 1911, the small,
oddly shaped plot that separated the
Conservatory from the YMCA. In the spring
of 1927, the school's trustees agreed to
build. George W. Brown, their president,
began the round of fund-raising by
donating $400,000 for a new hall. The fami-
ly of the recently deceased President Carr
seconded Brown's efforts, giving a splendid
organ room decorated in the rich orna-
mentation of early Spain.

For the new hall, Chadwick and Brown chose as their architects the firm of Haven and Hoyt. They produced an Italianate vision, with a ceiling modeled on Mantua's famous hall. As one enthusiast overexclaimed, "Veronese himself would not be ashamed" of the adorned ceiling, subtle walls, warm wood, and gleaming fixtures. The whole was "consciously designed to be analogous to musical harmonies."

Dedicated on December 10, 1929, the new hall, with removable seating, was named after its most generous supporter: George Brown. It made not only a fine auditorium but also a stage, lecture hall, and ballroom for the round of waltzes, fox-trots, and Charlestons that were to grace the next decade. For the next sixty years, Brown Hall served the Conservatory as refectory, stage, recital hall, and meeting place. Students have run through its corridors, practiced in its quiet alcoves, and marveled at its acoustics.

President Brown did not live to see his vision come to life. On November 16, 1928, he died at the age of eighty-three. To the very end he remained active in school affairs. For six years he had served as president, succeeding Samuel Carr in 1922 and continuing the tradition of active trustee leadership. Like Eben Jordan, Sr., he had been a self-made man; like Eben Jordan, Jr., his first love had always been music. As a child, he had shown genuine musical talent, but his father had wanted a practical man. He was that too. Starting virtually from scratch, he had built the United Shoe Machinery Company into one of America's most prosperous industries. Yet he had never lost his love for music. He became a Conservatory trustee, sent his daughter to study there, and treasured the memory of her performances with its orchestra. She died young. Bowed by the tragedy, he endowed a violin scholarship in her memory. To the end of his days, his most treasured memento was a photograph taken of her at the Conservatory, holding her violin.

After Brown's death, Chadwick remained at the helm for only another year. On December 4, 1930, he retired having served as director for thirty-three years. Soon after his appointment in 1897, he had written of his hopes "to develop a school on broad artistic lines which will be a power in the land." As he conceded, such a plan required of him "very little teaching and much scheming and planning." He had done that and more. He had transformed an impoverished piano and voice academy into a modern conservatory. That work made him the most important figure in the school's history.

Then he retired to his home on Martha's Vineyard, but not before his conservatory had honored him with a Chadwick Commemorative. On May 6, 1930, the orchestra he had created performed the music he had composed on the fiftieth anniversary of his first great success: the debut of his *Rip Van Winkle* in 1880. It was a great celebration of all that Chadwick meant to NEC. Less than a year later, his old friend and successor, Wallace Goodrich, undertook a more melancholy duty. For Chadwick died on April 4, 1931, and the Conservatory staged a sad farewell: the Chadwick Memorial Concert of May 19, 1931. Chosen and conducted by Goodrich, the program encompassed Chadwick's life and influence. Music by Bach and Brahms reiterated to the tradition that had nurtured Chadwick. Selections from Horatio Parker and the contemporary French composer Chausson indicated how Chadwick, in turn, had enriched and passed along that tradition. As if verifying his work in popularizing important music, WBJ, the local affiliate of the NBC Radio Network, broadcast the concert.

Far from Jordan Hall at NEC, though, other sounds already commanded the public's attention. Wall Street had crashed in 1929, casting down American prosperity and confidence in its wake. The looming Depression seemed remote from the rich warmth of Jordan Hall at NEC, but the Conservatory now had to find its way in the wake of the collapsing economy without its greatest leader.

POC
BILLIA
TABLE

CURTIS
SHOES

MONEY TO LOAL
S & A JEWELRY CO

36

MONEY TO LOAN | TRUNKS BAGS AND SUIT CASES | READY FOR RAILROAD WATCHES | JEWELRY DIAMONDS AND WEDDING RINGS | GIFTS CLOCKS SILVERWARE TOILET SETS | WE OLD SIL PLAT

S & A JEWELRY CO. OPTICAL REPA

S L JEWELRY CO DIAMONDS

36 WATCH REPAIRING

JOHN WALLACE GOODRICH: THE DEPRESSION YEARS

7

As for you, young fellow, you can fittingly quote, when you speak of the accomplishments and the qualities of the Conservatory (if you haven't forgotten your Virgil) "quorum pars magni gui." It was in a pretty damned bad way when you took over. Decay was setting in, the administering was not good, the books were spattered with red ink and the outlook was forbidding. You salvaged and regenerated and improved it physically and financially and spiritually.

—*Anonymous Trustee to*
President Philip Allen (1948)

Just as Goodrich took command of the Conservatory, the Depression cast a shadow over the entire country, and Bostonians became more concerned with food than music. Here, a bread line on Hanover Street in the North End, 1931.

Chadwick boasted that he had "'clawed off the lee shore' as the sailors say." Under his direction, New England Conservatory had built one of the nation's finest concert halls, developed a modern curriculum, awarded its first baccalaureates, and staked its place in classical music. It had also turned a profit every year for the last three decades, even, Chadwick reminded his trustees, "during the anxious years of the war."

So the school plumped for more of the same. When George Brown died in 1928, trustees chose his son, Edwin, to succeed him as president. When Chadwick retired in 1930, they named John Wallace Goodrich as director. Although almost sixty, Goodrich was the obvious choice: he had succeeded Chadwick as conductor of the Worcester Music Festival in 1902, filled in as acting director of NEC in 1905–6, served as dean of NEC since 1907, conducted the unhappy Boston Opera Company from 1908–11, and became the regular conductor of the NEC Orchestra in 1919.

A large man hailing from Newton, Massachusetts, Goodrich cultivated a huge walrus mustache and at the time displayed the energy of a dervish. For more than thirty-five years, he had lived out his musical career at the Conservatory in Chadwick's shadow. He had studied with Chadwick, followed his trail to Munich and Rheinberger, returned to teach organ at Franklin Square, and settled into administration and teaching. His once-promising musical career evolved into a professional pedagogic routine, with spare time for frequent rounds of golf.

But he was not prepared for the crises that swept through his Conservatory. Just as he put his hand to the tiller, America smashed up against the worst economic depression in its history. Within three years of the Wall Street collapse, America's stocks lost more than 80 percent of their value. In the chaos and panic, some 4,300 banks failed. By 1933, more than thirteen million Americans were without jobs and without much hope of finding them. Also by 1933, and more perilously for NEC, an estimated 1,500 colleges had gone bankrupt and closed.

The Conservatory spun in the hurricane. After reaching 3,448 students in 1926, its enrollment fell, year after discouraging year. In 1931, fewer than 2,000 students registered; in 1934, only 1,453; in 1936, 1,383; in 1938, 1,344; in 1939, 1,340. By 1942, the school had only 1,165 students, and most of them were part-time or occasional pupils, taking a class or two to fill their idle time.

Plummeting enrollment wasn't the school's only worry. The money for which Chadwick had so assiduously begged over three decades now evaporated in the wake of the great crash. The school had expected to use bequests such as Samuel Carr's $50,000, Clara Kathleen Rogers's $10,000, and Albert Whiting's $15,000 to bridge the growing gap between income and costs, to prepare for future needs, and to provide scholarships for needy students. Now, they produced nothing at all. In December 1934, Goodrich acknowledged that the school was once again dangerously close to that lee shore. For the only time in the twentieth century, NEC was forced to suspend financial aid, "owing to the total cessation of income from the securities presented."

After twenty-five years of profit, the Conservatory again plunged into debt. The construction of Brown Hall left the trustees with a $200,000 mortgage for space they couldn't fill. Forced back into the deficits from which Chadwick had clawed free, the Conservatory began to borrow: in November 1931, the trustees took out a $40,000 loan to meet current expenses; in June 1934, they borrowed another $60,000; in 1936, $19,000, then another $2,000.

To clear up those tangled debts, they agreed to set up a "sustaining fund" of $100,000. That too failed. In less than a year, they conceded defeat, the campaign for such a fund had to be put off "until a more auspicious time for raising money." For now, they could only borrow and economize. Even the mortgage proved too much. Between 1932 and 1939, they barely met the interest payments. The principal remained unpaid.

The Conservatory also faced an unexpected challenge from new, and better-funded, music schools. In 1918, the nation's camera tycoon, George Eastman, sank $20 million into the University of Rochester's Eastman School of Music, transforming an obscure Institute of Musical Art into one of America's leading conservatories. In 1924, Mrs. Mary Curtis Bok, heir to the Curtis publishing fortune, bequeathed $12.5 million to make the Curtis Institute of Music one of the country's most lavishly endowed schools; after 1927 its students weren't even charged tuition. And New York's Institute of Musical Art merged with the richly endowed Juilliard Graduate School in 1926 to provide a third "rivalry."

As early as 1919, Chadwick had fretted over competitors, "whose resources are increasing and whose methods are often modeled upon those of this institution." To meet the challenge, he put his faith in dormitories, financial aid, and advertising. But in the straitened circumstances of the 1930s, Goodrich was forced to slash operating costs and reduce, or eliminate, every item on his predecessors' agenda.

Advertising went first. Goodrich felt a Puritan's disapproval for what he called "paid publicity." So he cut the budget entirely. That saved a few dollars but left the field to Eastman, Curtis, and Juilliard.

Then he went after the residence halls. Goodrich shared Chadwick's dislike of dormitories, and he wanted to get rid of them. For four years they had been a drain on his budget, so in 1935 he shut down Dana, Frost, and Gardner halls, moved residents into the nearby Boston Students' Union, and offered the property to Tufts for its growing medical school. But Tufts faced financial problems of its own. When the university reluctantly backed away, the buildings remained closed while Goodrich spent the next five years looking frantically—and unsuccessfully—for a buyer.

As a third cost-cutting measure, Goodrich stopped giving scholarships. He saw financial assistance as "a moral privilege," rather than an educational inducement. He insisted that scholarships only inhibited a student's "sense of appreciation and of obligation and of qualities of initiative and self-reliance." So he stressed loans, calculating that their "eventual repayment" would make better use of the school's dwindling funds. But such measures, thrifty in the short term, served only to erode NEC's place among America's conservatories. Finally, even Goodrich recognized that. "The answer," he told trustees, "must be endowment."

His new president, Philip Allen, agreed. Allen had succeeded Edwin Brown in 1934. A Yale-educated manufacturer and banker, Allen possessed an enthusiasm for music that reminded veterans of the days of Eben Jordan. He was not only a member of Boston's Federal Reserve but also a student at NEC. At sixty-two, he had taken up the cello, studying with the BSO's Alfred Zighera. One of the few who did not need scholarship money, Allen nevertheless recognized that most students did.

In January 1937, Allen organized a $3 million endowment drive to meet the mortgage, pay off the accumulated debts, establish pensions for faculty and staff, repair the deteriorating buildings, and provide scholarships. He envisioned a massive, long-term effort that might settle the school's finances forever. But, like Chadwick's effort in 1917, that one also failed. Chadwick had launched his appeal on the brink of war, then watched helplessly as it sank in the wake of the Lusitania.

Now Goodrich and Allen revived his strategy. Their drive ran into an economy where some twenty million Americans lived hand-to-mouth. Raising money for future musicians seemed a luxury beyond popular imagination. After only two months of unsuccessful begging, they conceded defeat. The trustees agreed that the Conservatory was not yet "in a strong enough position to warrant seeking an endowment at this time."

Goodrich staggered on as best he could. With no help to cover falling revenues, he cut costs ruthlessly. He stopped publication of the school's *Bulletin*, ended subsidies for the in-residence Boston String Quartet, closed the Drama School, cut back on piano rentals, deferred much-needed repairs, dismissed staff, and delayed all talk of pensions. He even ended the Mason and Hamlin Competition so that he would not have to award a prize. And he cut salaries as close to the bone as he dared: in 1932 he reduced teachers' salaries by 10 percent; two years later, he slashed them another 25 percent. He did not pretend that they could afford it but pleaded "the necessity of balancing the budget." There were no other jobs, so the faculty stayed on, scanned the economy, and sacrificed. Goodrich and the trustees acknowledged their "fine spirit of cooperation" but worried about their gang of threadbare, hungry, and discouraged teachers.

Goodrich also worried about the edifice Chadwick had created. Desperately short of money, Goodrich delayed repairs until they became critical or someone offered to pay for them. He authorized $5,400 for roof repairs only when the rain started pouring in, and $500 for a new Jordan Hall boiler only after the old one burned out. Trustees chipped in $783 to replace Jordan Hall at NEC's curtains when the old ones became too shabby to use.

A much-needed refurbishing of the entire hall was deferred until 1938, when a ladies' group headed by Pauline Fenno took on the work and the expense. They collected enough money to paint Jordan Hall at NEC, re-cover its seats, and lay down new, considerably brighter carpeting. At last, audiences no longer needed to fear those dark stairs. Fenno and her committee staved off deterioration for the moment, ensuring that Jordan Hall at NEC remained a place worthy of its music.

Despite the cuts and delays, Goodrich couldn't make ends meet. In 1934, the school suffered its worst loss so far: $60,000. Goodrich slashed everything in sight but succeeded only in steadying a listing ship. All he could do was "reduce operating loss to a minimum" while revenues continued to fall. In 1941 the Conservatory lost more than $9,000; in 1942, more than $35,000. By then, America had once more entered into war. The trustees recognized that "great thrift will be necessary for the duration."

To save his school, Goodrich turned to government aid and musical innovation. He was ambivalent about both. Ever the traditionalist and Yankee Republican, he nevertheless inched his way forward. A lifetime in Boston had taught him to be wary of government intervention. The vagaries of patronage politics worried him, and he feared that music would be stamped out by some New Deal machine. He opposed Congress's effort to establish a Federal Bureau of the Arts, since for him that meant "nationalized" music, conforming to political and bureaucratic, rather than artistic, standards.

Yet he endorsed less-ambitious aspects of President Roosevelt's New Deal. In 1935 he joined the executive of the new Works Progress Administration (WPA)'s musical program, becoming one of the first music educators to do so. And he recruited allies, enlisting the celebrated pianist Lee Pattison and his old colleague Arthur Shepherd to work with him. With their assistance, the WPA doled out grants to composers, singers, bands, and orchestras for musical projects ranging from recording traditional blues to commissioning new works. Ambitious, frustrating, spreading too few dollars through the ranks of needy artists and performers, the WPA nevertheless marked the government's first fitful steps toward support for the arts. It also encouraged the hope that, when the country finally found its feet again, artists and musicians would have survived.

Goodrich organized a WPA orchestra in Boston, and by 1938, seventeen members of the school's orchestra earned their tuition playing for the government. Scheduling conflicts among those part-time professionals drove Goodrich to distraction, but he also understood that there were few jobs out there, and that they desperately needed the money to stay in school, develop their talents, and play for him.

One government project, however, proved an unmixed blessing for his Conservatory. As early as 1934, Goodrich had argued that the school might "derive benefit" from the coming Federal Emergency Relief Administration (FERA), and events justified his hopes. Although FERA—renamed the Federal Youth Administration—was denounced as a "dole," it offered students financial aid in return for "performing service." And the Conservatory, deteriorating year by year, desperately needed that service. Within a year, thirty-five students were working for tuition money, repairing books and music, cataloguing the school's library, and performing in the Boston area.

WPA, FERA, NYA, and other New Deal programs helped some of America's impoverished and unemployed. For the rest, there was nothing to do but tighten the belt another notch and wait for the return of better times. Goodrich and his students longed for the good old days. According to a survey by NEC's *Bulletin*, the students' favorite performers were the heirs—or the stars—of the nineteenth century: Kreisler, Paderewski, and Rachmaninoff. Their favorite composers were from the old guard as well. The typical student, according to the survey, "adores Beethoven, dislikes crooning and hopes to marry a non-musician."

Goodrich, as a traditionalist, a church-educated composer, and a conductor, recognized that the Conservatory had to move with the times or disappear. So he turned it toward musical innovation. First, he seized upon technology to enhance both education and performance. He begged and borrowed the paraphernalia of a modern music studio, welcoming not only the donation of a used Victrola and old records but also a secondhand "talking machine," which, he confessed, "we are

endeavoring to induce to function…without conspicuous success." Those were humble beginnings: Goodrich invited students to use the "rather 'spotty' collection of records" anytime they wanted—so long as it was "between the hours of one and two daily." But records accumulated, more Victrolas appeared, and in 1939 the trustees agreed to spend $600 on a recording studio, complete with a Steinway and "the most up-to-date equipment." Goodrich even dipped into his own depleted funds for this expensive, but inevitable, addition.

He also championed radio performances. Under Chadwick, Conservatory ensembles had dipped into the possibilities of broadcasting. Now Goodrich eagerly plunged into the ether. Three weeks after becoming director, he conducted the NEC Orchestra in a half-hour broadcast over WNAC, commemorated Chadwick's death with another broadcast over WBJ, and concluded his first year with a performance of Converse's *Mystic Trumpeter*, broadcast by WHDH. NBC aired two of his 1933 concerts nationally. By the end of the year, he had arranged for regular broadcasts on Boston's WBZ. In 1935 he engineered a deal with WNAC, providing for weekly concerts by various Conservatory groups. In 1938 he moved to NBC, which offered occasional national broadcasts over its prestigious—though now forgotten—Blue Network. And in 1939 he added five national performances on CBS, including two beamed abroad by shortwave radio. Those programs introduced NEC's musicians to national audiences, revived alumni memories of Huntington Avenue, and provided an alternative to the advertising Goodrich could not afford. They also heartened students deeply discouraged by the prospects of employment in the failing economy.

Faced by an economic disaster, Goodrich focused on the music and education he knew so well. He improved the music curriculum by introducing courses in music criticism and technique, including one "to cure students of stage fright," another to teach the "vitally important" methods of "singing over the radio" and "singing and acting for the sound films," and a third to develop "recording and broadcasting technique."

In 1933 he introduced the Master of
Music program. It played only a minor role
during those difficult years: in the first
decade only twenty-five students received
the degree. But it marked the school's
commitment to professional levels of performance and research. It also brought a
few more dollars into the empty coffers and
set an ambitious course for the future.

Goodrich denounced the decline in
the quality of string players. He traced it to
two of America's most popular pastimes:
football, which led inevitably to "the
glorification of the band, with its opportunities to make itself heard at football
games," and radio and dance orchestras,
which he insisted aired their "stolid
indifference to the artistic value of stringed
instruments." Yet he decided to accompany,
rather than shout down, the modern
sounds coming from America's dance halls
and gridirons. He launched both a
Conservatory Band and a Program of
Popular Music, pledging both to the highest
"artistic standards of instrumentation,
repertoire and performance." By emphasizing "artistic" modern music, he calmed
the trustees, who hoped (as one confessed)
"that the style of inartistic singing on
certain radio programs would be discouraged in our school." Although Goodrich
walked a fine line between popular music
and "inartistic" performance, both the
band and popular music department helped
carry the Conservatory through hard
times. The band began humbly enough, but

it was something of an anachronism, harking back to the brass ensembles of Patrick Gilmore and John Philip Sousa, rather than to the swing bands that dominated radio, record sales, and dance floors. Goodrich insisted on "artistic results" and derived satisfaction when alumnus William Santlemann was named director of the United States Marine Band in 1940.

He sold his idea for a Program of Popular Music to suspicious trustees by focusing on composition and arrangement. The director, Ruby Newman, combined classical training as a violinist at the Mozarteum with more contemporary credentials. Voted "America's No. 1 Society Orchestra Leader" by *Swing* magazine, he was a veteran of Radio City's famous Rainbow Room. Newman's popular music program attracted a new kind of musician to the Conservatory and encouraged its hesitant steps toward a new and all-encompassing idea of American music. In his first year, Newman enrolled sixty students. Even during the dark days of the Second World War, he managed to find seventy-five students a year, though overall enrollments continued to fall.

With those lucrative ventures in hand, Goodrich set himself a more traditional and congenial task. He brought back opera. As dean and sometime conductor, he had long championed Conservatory opera, leading its first full performance in 1906. After the ignominious failure of the Boston Opera Company, he continued to present occasional operas. In 1925 he conducted students and alumni in Engelbert Humperdinck's *Hänsel und Gretel* at the Opera House. A year later, he returned with the more lavish *Madama Butterfly*, with NEC alumna (and future trustee) Jeska Swartz Morse as Suzuki. In 1928 he not only conducted Act II of *Faust*, with Cecile Sherman (yet another promising Conservatory alumna) as Marguerite, but also produced a program of orchestral excerpts.

Such efforts, and a few comic student performances, convinced him that he might manage the "well-nigh insoluble" problems of opera. Cautiously he approached opera from its lighter, less expensive side, beginning with a School of Opera, which he organized in the summer of 1936.

After that, too, failed, Goodrich finally got things moving when, in October 1940, he brought in George Reeves, former conductor of Covent Garden, to lead a course in opera ensemble. In April 1941, Goodrich found the money for Reeves to produce a concert version of Monteverdi's *Orfeo*, then a neglected work with only two American performances in thirty years. A year later, they presented two short works in English: Pergolesi's *Serva Padrona* and Puccini's *Suor Angelica*. His was the first Boston performance of Pergolesi's little drama, and the first of Puccini's in twenty years.

A more ambitious scheme, however, was already in the wings. In February 1942, Goodrich won trustee approval for a real opera school, with Boris Goldovsky as director. Only thirty-four, Goldovsky, like Koussevitzky, had fled the Soviet regime. After an education in Berlin and Budapest, he came to America in 1930, where he worked first in Philadelphia, then with the Cleveland Institute of Music's opera department and Berkshire Music Center's opera program. Balding and chubby, he was already a notorious storyteller who recounted adventures in any one of a half-dozen languages, with accompanying accents.

But he had good credentials, an enthusiastic endorsement from Koussevitzky, and great ambition. While opera was then in eclipse, he predicted "a growth in operatic productions similar to the great recent growth in symphonic performances and number of orchestras." In his own way, he contributed much to fulfill that dream.

Next page: NEC students perform Hänsel und Gretel *at the Boston Opera House in 1925.*

Eleanor Steber

Eleanor Steber liked to call herself the "little girl from Wheeling, West Virginia." Her soprano was anything but little. Her tenure as leading prima donna at the Metropolitan Opera, from 1940 to 1962, included thirty-three roles, but she was best known in her fifty-years-plus career for her interpretation of Mozart. In her later years, she was head of the voice department of the Cleveland Institute of Music. One of the Conservatory's most celebrated alumnae, Steber studied with William Whitney.

He opened his NEC Opera School in September 1942 under the worst possible conditions. Goodrich lacked money, so he hired Goldovsky part-time, paying him a mere $2,500. Then Goodrich promptly resigned, leaving his employee at the mercy of a new director, Quincy Porter. The trustees were wary of Goldovsky, too: while Popular Music received five $100 scholarships, the Opera School got only three for $45. And for the first three years, it averaged just thirty-four students, half as many as Popular Music. America was then at war, so trustees urged their new impresario to hurry a "small" production onto the stage by Christmas, "as the draft will affect us even more adversely later in the year." They also warned him that the orchestra was failing fast.

Goldovsky plunged ahead, keeping his school afloat by sheer enthusiasm. Although he missed Christmas, he staged a performance in February 1943, after only five months at Huntington Avenue. Like Bimboni before him, he opted for a program of miscellaneous scenes: parts of Tchaikovsky's *Eugene Onegin*, selections from Offenbach's *Mariage aux Lanternes*, and the death scene from *Aïda*. He not only coached, directed, produced, and conducted those performances but translated each of the three works into his own vivid English. The orchestra, down to some fifty musicians, did its best to keep pace: in his first year, he presented scenes from thirty-three operas, with forty-two of the Conservatory's singers on the Jordan Hall stage.

Nevertheless, Goldovsky's ambitions extended far beyond Jordan's stage. Less a teacher than an old-fashioned impresario, he wanted to make a place for opera in America's cultural life. So, in January 1945, with the war in Europe winding down, he launched a New England Opera Theater, "under the sponsorship of the New England Conservatory." In 1946 he took an additional job as master of ceremonies for the Metropolitan Opera Company's intermission radio show "Opera on the Air." That ideally suited his talent for explanation, enthusiasm, and penchant for multilingual non sequiturs. Audiences loved him. He wore his many hats with characteristic energy, producing *The Marriage of Figaro* in November 1946 under the combined auspices of the Conservatory, the New England Opera Theater, and the Goldovsky Opera Institute.

The third leg of Goodrich's program of musical innovation provided support for contemporary music. In his early years, he had been something of an experimentalist, conducting not only the works of Chadwick and Converse but more difficult pieces by such modernists as Vaughan Williams, César Franck, and his longtime friend Gabriel Fauré. Only in the 1920s had he drifted back to the conventional repertoire, compelled by the need to move his orchestra through the late-nineteenth-century repertoire before he could expect it to understand the moderns.

JORDAN HALL
WEDNESDAY EVENING, MARCH 2, 1938, AT 8:30 O'CLOCK

INFORMAL LECTURE
by
NADIA BOULANGER
ON WORKS OF
CLAUDIO MONTEVERDI

❧❧

Assisting:

Mmes.	Jean de Polignac	Irène Kédroff
	Gisèle Peyron	Nathalie Kédroff
Mm.	Hugues Cuénod	Doda Conrad

❧❧

Illustrations

1. Hor ch'el ciel
    Lamento della Ninfa
    Lasciatemi morire

2. Ecco mormorar l'onde

3. Romanesca
    Chiome d'oro

4. Ballo dell' Ingrate

Genevieve Thompson, Florence Chapman, *violin*
Sally Dodge, Elizabeth Darling, *viola*
Dorothy Jump, Adelaide Hubbard, *violoncello*
Margaret Alvord, *contrabass*

*In 1938, French composer and conductor
Nadia Boulanger performed in Jordan Hall
at NEC at Goodrich's request.*

To help his students understand contemporary music, Goodrich brought in three powerful exponents of this new aesthetic. In January 1934, Sergei Radamsky, former NEC student and champion of the new wave of Russian composers, returned to Jordan Hall at NEC, where he sang much of that music before a sold-out crowd to benefit Icor, one of the first organizations aiding Jews in the Soviet Union. In March 1938 Chadwick welcomed Nadia Boulanger. Post-war American composers had gone to her as their predecessors had to Rheinberger. Her American Conservatory at Fontainebleau was that generation's Munich. She had been a friend and disciple to Fauré and Stravinsky, as well as teacher to such American talents as Aaron Copland, David Diamond, and Walter Piston. But to her overflowing audience in Jordan Hall at NEC, she preached the genius of another, and perhaps more unfamiliar, composer: Monteverdi. Her enthusiasm for the neglected Italian masters of the seventeenth century not only helped to revive interest in Baroque music but steered a new generation of students away from the traditional German repertoire. And when Quincy Porter arrived to take up his duties as the new dean of the faculty in 1938, Goodrich took one look at his compositions and put him down for an utterly new class: A Survey of Contemporary Music. At last the new names—Stravinsky, Webern, Copland, and even Schoenberg—appeared, if not in Jordan Hall at NEC, at least in its adjacent classrooms.

*in faithful remembrance of so many happy hours
in Jordan Hall
To my dear friend Wallace Goodrich*

Nadia Boulanger

23 July 1949

Goodrich's mixture of contemporary American and French music became a signature of his concerts. In May 1935 he offered the world premiere of George Newell's *Rio Bravo* and the American debut of Gaubert's *Les Chants de Mer*. That October, he gave his audience Bach, as well as Charles Martin Loeffler and Saint-Saëns. And in November 1937 he revived both Converse's *Concertino* and—after thirty years—Franck's *Psyché*. Determined to expand his orchestra's repertoire, he conducted Corelli and Rachmaninoff as well as Frederick Converse and Carl McKinley.

He also gave the new generation of composers and audiences its first opportunity to hold the Jordan Hall stage. On May 21, 1942, he handed over his hall and orchestra to a dynamic young conductor eager to play modern music. The piece was Aaron Copland's *Second Hurricane*, a stagy two-act opera mixing modern ideas of tonality with equally modern thoughts on race relations. And the conductor, praised by the *Globe* for moving a talky opera "briskly through its course," was Leonard Bernstein, who had taken piano lessons at NEC. His affection for modern music was to educate audience's understanding for a generation, but not that night. Although Copland attended the performance, few others did. Critics complained that the audience was "not so large as it ought to have been."

The concert, with its promising young conductor and its dedication to modern music, signaled a change in the life of Jordan Hall at NEC and the Conservatory. Goodrich seemed to sense as much. Three weeks later, he handed in his resignation, effective July 1, 1942. He was succeeded by the modernist he had taken aboard in 1938: Quincy Porter. Goodrich deserved his rest and his golf. He had never attained the stature of Chadwick, but he had nursed the Conservatory through a dangerous period in its history, keeping a faint pulse in an ailing institution.

Quincy Porter, who succeeded Wallace Goodrich as director in 1938, continued the Conservatory's direction toward modernism.

He left behind not only a changing repertoire but a changed Conservatory. No longer just a singing school, it was becoming a training ground for orchestral musicians. The link that Faelten had first forged with Gericke and the BSO had been galvanized by Goodrich's work with Serge Koussevitzky. In 1939, twenty-three alumni played for the BSO, while twenty-one of the BSO musicians taught at the Conservatory. Koussevitzky not only conducted an unusually large number of compositions by Conservatory faculty (such as Chadwick and Converse) but judged the school's Mason and Hamlin Prize, trained twenty-seven of its students in his first year at Tanglewood, and joined its Board of Trustees in 1944.

The tie with the BSO, though, was only a part of the school's success: alumni also worked as conductors of the Kansas City Philharmonic and the Houston Symphony Orchestra, assistant conductor of the Cleveland Orchestra, and director of the Women's Symphony Orchestra in Boston. They dominated the Houston Symphony Orchestra, holding eleven chairs. They also filled three each in St. Louis, Minneapolis, Cincinnati, Cleveland, and Indianapolis; two in Chicago, Detroit, and Rochester; one in Philadelphia, Kansas City, and Washington. More than half of the Women's Orchestra were also NEC students, still struggling to find conductors who responded to talent, rather than tradition.

The NEC community filled prestigious positions in American orchestras and circled the globe. Two graduates staffed the music department of Ewha Haktung in Seoul, the only women's college in Korea. There Mary Young and Laura Ye continued the commitment to women's education and rights that stretched back to those suffragette rallies. Another alumnus, Bliss Wiant, pursued similar work in Beijing, where he headed the Christian Yenching College's music program and for Christmas 1935 conducted Handel's *Messiah* in a troubled city.

For war had come to China. The long, terrible struggle between an expansionist Japan and its prostrate neighbor had already begun. Idella Chow, another NEC graduate, saw in Beijing "the fear of enemies…Every day more troops… Japanese army planes and bombers fly over the city." Yet she stayed, teaching piano at Bridgman Academy, educating a generation of Chinese women only recently freed from foot binding.

For NEC, such work meant more than fantastic letters from the far corners of the earth. Well before Pearl Harbor, international politics had again come to the Conservatory. Opportunities in defense work and the requirements of America's first peacetime draft further reduced enrollments. Students who remained read about the London Blitz, performed for the British War Relief, and waited for America to go to war.

The Women's Symphony Orchestra of Boston, performing its inaugural concert at Symphony Hall, was a lifesaver for the many NEC women graduates hard-pressed to find work in the country's predominately male orchestras.

When it did, Conservatory students again rallied to the cause. As they had in 1917, NEC's musicians went to war. For those who stayed, Huntington Avenue was a grim place. Goodrich, followed by Quincy Porter and, later, his assistant and dean, Malcolm Holmes, struggled to keep their orchestra going "under the present difficult war-time conditions." It was hard work. By 1944 strings and woodwinds had disappeared into the army. The orchestra was reduced to a band of fewer than fifty musicians, playing only three concerts a year. It looked as though Chadwick's legacy was about to fail. But administrators cajoled alumni into retaking old chairs. Porter and Holmes conducted small ensembles through musical excerpts in a cold, nearly empty Jordan Hall at NEC. "The orchestra," Porter confessed in his first report to the trustees, "has dwindled so much due to complete lack of woodwind instrumentalists that it cannot function for commencement exercises."

In 1942 the Conservatory had to cancel not only the Commencement Concert but Commencement itself. Brown Hall was shut, studios closed, and oil and electricity strictly rationed. Elderly teachers, called out of retirement to fill thinning faculty ranks, fell asleep in the middle of their own lessons. Students shuttled between classes and air-raid drills. Fifty years later, one pianist's most vivid memory was "freezing fingers right before piano lesson (Opus 111)!" Even occasional efforts to escape the dreary regimen were overtaken by the war: the Undergraduate Dance of 1942 collapsed when Boston officials declared a civil-defense blackout in the middle of the jitterbug. Yet, as Quincy Porter reminded the trustees in 1944, "Our school has not suffered as badly as a great majority."

The sudden upheaval was laconically summarized by one alumnus fifty years later: "Completed program in 1942—then into the Army." He did not go alone. A year after Pearl Harbor, ninety-six students, as well as five staff, had entered the service; by the end of the war, 318 students, alumni, teachers, and administrators—including more than a dozen women—had served in the armed forces. The *Globe* expressed mild surprise in its headline that "New England Conservatory Students Show 'Teamwork in National Service!'" But they did what a nation fighting a total war on four continents asked, becoming radio operators, infantrymen and combat instructors, artillerymen and airplane pilots. Students joined the artillery in North Africa, the marines in Guadalcanal, the army in Sicily, or the Air Corps over Greece. Seven Conservatory men died in the fighting. Captain Clarence Corning, the enthusiastic publicist who had organized the failed 1937 endowment drive, spent two years in a German POW camp.

For a few students, the war provided an outlet for their music. One Conservatory student found himself in Norfolk, singing with the Naval Chorus and meeting Douglas Fairbanks, Jr. Another directed an army band whose performances were broadcast over the oddly named new BBC program, "Yankee Follies."

A captured Japanese submarine on Tremont Street decorated with a war bond advertisement. For NEC, World War II meant a pitiful orchestra on the brink of disappearing, as the string and woodwind sections joined the army.

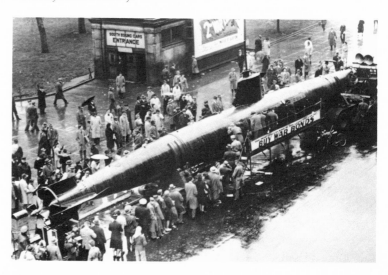

For most, though, the war was merely a terrible lacuna between school and career, whether they spent it singing in a Virginia chorus, "living in fox-holes…and suffering all the hardships of the jungle" or (as one volunteer lamented) "playing tuba in an understrength band in Australia."

They returned to a country that was already changing. The war had swept away not only Fascist Europe and militarist Japan but the last vestiges of depression America. Now a victorious, prosperous, and confident country welcomed its veterans home, then sought to provide for them. The Conservatory was ready. By September 1944 enrollment had doubled to 2,314, including forty veterans, the highest number of students since 1929. Even then, the government was preparing the most important legislation in the history of higher education: Public Law 346 (later the G.I. Bill), which paid for veterans' education and, in one generation, transformed college from a bastion of privilege into a road for advancement.

By December 1945, 114 veterans had enrolled at NEC, most of them as "full-course" students and "all under the auspices of the Federal government." In the next year, hundreds more flocked in, including forty former students who had been drafted out of Huntington Avenue. Enrollment bounced back to the extraordinary levels of the 1920s and included large numbers of "full-course" students preparing for degrees. Fifty percent of them were veterans.

Those were great days. The Conservatory had survived depression and war. NEC was suddenly hard-pressed to find room for all its new students. It was the first time the Conservatory turned away serious musicians because it was unable to accommodate them. The Opera and Popular Music schools flourished, the dormitories came out of mothballs, and the number of ensembles exploded. Goldovsky threw himself into a full-scale production of Mozart's *Figaro*, the newly hired Barry Greene tried to create a chorus, and a young theory teacher named Chester Williams found himself teaching thirty-five hours of Introductory Solfège each week. By the fall of 1946, the school had a band, a 175-voice chorus, as well as two popular and three symphony orchestras.

The main orchestra, once reduced to a remnant of student musicians barely able to eke out a couple of performances a year, grew and flourished. Under Quincy Porter and Dean Malcolm Holmes, it continued to experiment with newer works, presenting Shostakovich's First Symphony, Prokofiev's *Classical Symphony*, Glazunov's Concerto for Violin, a Fauré festival, and, in a bow to a much-loved member of the faculty, Ernst Lévy's *Elégie Française*. In December 1945, Holmes rallied his small ensemble to perform two Boston premieres for its first peacetime concert: David Diamond's Rounds for Strings and Ellis Kohs's Concerto for Orchestra. In October 1946 he conducted the first local performance of Vaughan Williams's *Dives and Lazarus*.

The great days meant financial as well as musical success. For the first time in its history, the Conservatory paid off all its debt. Rising enrollment ended the need for humiliating loans and produced unprecedented revenues, which were used to retire the old mortgage. By 1945 that had fallen to only $50,000; by December 13, 1946, it had been paid off entirely. That gave President Allen an opportunity to realize two ambitions he had set for himself twelve years before. First, he announced plans for a new $3 million endowment drive. Then, as fellow trustees gathered around, he put a match to the mortgage. Together they watched as the last evidence of their debt, and their years of struggle, curled up in flames.

In the wake of the Great War, America listened to jazz, but it would be several decades before the Conservatory started its jazz studies program, in the 1960s.

NEC students perform Ariadne auf Naxos, *February 1951.*

GOLDOVSKY AND MILLER: THE CONSERVATORY'S STAR MAKERS

Boris Goldovsky opened the NEC Opera School in 1942 and trained a generation of opera stars.

Voice teacher Gladys Miller inspired countless vocalists during her fifty-year tenure at NEC.

Despite the fickle state of the Conservatory's opera program during its early days, New England Conservatory managed to produce several opera luminaries, most notably Lillian Norton (1875), known worldwide as "Nordica," and Eleanor Steber (1938), star of the Metropolitan Opera. But the Conservatory's most fruitful era for vocalists came during the forties and fifties, when Boris Goldovsky headed the opera workshop and Gladys Miller was fully entrenched in her career as a voice teacher. Their musical wisdom and talent for teaching influenced a generation of singers.

As Master of Ceremonies at the Metropolitan Opera Company's "Opera on the Air", Goldovsky's vibrant personality became well-known throughout the country. In 1954, he was recognized with a Peabody Award for Outstanding Contribution to Radio Music for his "contagious enthusiasm and the joy he experiences sharing his knowledge of opera." During that era, he was America's principal champion of opera as theater.

Phyllis Curtin

But it was as head of the opera workshop at NEC, a post he took on in 1942, that Goldovsky had the most lasting influence. Under his tutelage, dozens of young singers blossomed into opera stars embraced by both America and Europe. Goldovsky also brightened the Boston opera scene, which, when he came, he found dormant. He created the New England Opera Theater in 1946, offering a venue for his talented students. One of them was Sarah Caldwell (1946).

Sarah Caldwell

Caldwell stopped playing violin to pursue opera because of Goldovsky, the "white knight of opera" she called him; later she assisted him with the New England Opera Theater. When that company floundered, she formed her own, the Opera Group of Boston (later called the Opera Company of Boston) in 1957. For many years, it was Boston's only opera company, bringing in such names as Beverly Sills, Marilyn Horne, and Placido Domingo. Caldwell also became the first woman conductor for the Metropolitan Opera, an honor that landed her on the front cover of *Time Magazine*.

Goldovsky-trained singer Phyllis Curtin (1949), known for her interpretations of Mozart, appeared as a leading soprano for the Vienna Staatsoper, La Scala, and Teatro Colon, in addition to the Metropolitan Opera. Goldovsky first discovered her in 1946 during the Tanglewood summer opera program he supervised. She studied with him at NEC and become one of the many singers Goldovsky said he "invented." Later she appeared in the first opera Sarah Caldwell directed, Vaughan Williams's *Riders to the Sea,* and became artist in residence and teacher of the Phyllis Curtin Seminar and Vocal Fellows at Tanglewood, attracting students from across the world. From 1983 to 1991 she headed Boston University's School of the Arts.

Rosalind Elias

Yet another Metropolitan Opera star, Rosalind Elias (1951) was influenced by Goldovsky. Elias, a mezzo-soprano, joined the Met in 1958, and she spent several summers with Goldovsky at Tanglewood. In addition to the Met, Elias performed with the opera companies of San Francisco and Boston, as well as with the Paris Opera, the Teatro San Carlo, and the Vienna Staatsoper. She also developed a significant career as an opera stage director.

But Elias's success owes itself only partly to Goldovsky. At the Conservatory, Elias's guiding light was her voice teacher Gladys Miller.

Miller, whose first connection with the conservatory was when she sang Handel's *Messiah* in a presentation conducted by George Chadwick, was a beloved faculty member of the Conservatory for fifty years. So cherished was she that in 1973 several alumni set up a scholarship fund in her name, the Gladys Childs Miller Scholarship Fund, "to commemorate and honor Miss Miller for her fifty years of effective teaching and relations with students."

Said Chester Williams: "She had the ability to make each student feel the most important student of the day." Lacking a set system, Miller treated each student differently, never imposing her own style. "All the voice students wanted Gladys," said Williams. "She could never say no to them. Her only way out was to tell them, 'You'll have to speak with President Williams.'" Her devotion to her students revealed itself during their performances, when she would sit in the back of Jordan Hall and mouth the words along with them.

D'Anna Fortunato

Lucy Shelton

Miller's influence spanned many decades. Lucy Shelton (1968 M.M.) and D'Anna Fortunato (1968, 1970 M.M., 1972 A.D.) were two of her last students. Shelton became known for her adventurous programming that spanned traditional to modern. She has given the world premieres of more than fifty pieces and is the only artist to have ever won the Naumburg Award twice. In 1980, she was named "the future of the song recital," by the *New York Times*. Miller, she says, "was an absolutely wonderful eccentric teacher."

D'Anna Fortunato has appeared as a concert and oratorio soloist with the Chamber Music Society of Lincoln Center and Musica Sacra and has had leading roles with the New York City Opera, the Opera Company of Boston, and Glimmerglass Opera. She vividly remembers her daily lessons with Miller. "She had a combination of wonderful intuition, an incredible amount of experience with repertoire, and personality," she says. "You could always feel her presence in the school; you could feel her breathing with you, mouthing the words."

One of Miller's last public outings was at the premiere of Bizet's *Carmen* by the Lowell Opera Company. Miller watched as not only Rosalind Elias, the company's founder, but also four of her other former students performed. At the reception afterward, Miller shed tears for her joy at seeing her "kids" perform together. She passed away in 1978, but her presence remains with her students. Says Fortunato: "I still carry her around with me."

HARRISON KELLER:
GOOD TIMES AND BAD

8

It is not well to give a musical education to anyone who has nothing more than a mediocre talent…Therefore, the trustees are not to consider cases of mediocre talent…merely because such applicants declare themselves in need of help to pursue their studies.

—*Bequest of Clara Kathleen Rogers*

Full-time registration climbed to an all-time high in 1946, then climbed higher still the next year and the year after that. Talented students, and tuition dollars, poured in. Finally, the school did not need to borrow or economize. Instead, it paid off old debts, introduced faculty raises and pensions, and provided new scholarships. Philip Allen put the finishing touches to his presidency by establishing reserve and unrestricted funds of almost $750,000, lest "the good times…not continue."

In 1956, new dormitories were built along Gainsborough Street, across from Jordan Hall at NEC, to replace the dilapidated buildings on Hemenway Street. In addition to housing accommodations, they featured a new library and cafeteria.

A new generation of students flooded in to make music. Thirty percent of them were veterans, paying their way on the G.I. Bill and bringing new ideas to Huntington Avenue. By 1947 the Popular Music Department had found a home for more than two hundred of them. Their concerts attracted huge, enthusiastic audiences and—according to the *Herald*—got "old Jordan Hall…jumping in a discreet sort of fashion."

The NEC Orchestra also took on new life. Malcolm Holmes, who had frantically struggled to keep up a ragged ensemble during the war, now conducted an orchestra of eighty-five and turned away still more. He drilled them in the standard repertoire, in new and unfamiliar works by such contemporary composers as Samuel Barber, Aaron Copland, David Diamond, and Walter Piston, and he even premiered works by the Conservatory's students.

Holmes wrote the book on educating young instrumentalists. His *Conducting an Amateur Orchestra*, published in 1951, drew upon his Conservatory work to argue for both preservation and growth of the classical repertoire. He revived neglected pieces and challenged his players with new ones. In 1949 he conducted the first Boston performance of Bruckner's impassioned *Mass*; in 1950, the first local presentation of Schumann's *Paradise and the Peri* in seventy-five years. In 1951 he conducted the first Festival of New England Music, tracing a thematic line from Paine and Chadwick through Arthur Shepherd and Arthur Foote to Carl McKinley and Leland Proctor. Conservatory students entertained Conservatory audiences with the works of former Conservatory students: Mabel Daniels, then 73 and the last of America's pioneering women composers, took a well-deserved bow for her *Deep Forest*. McKinley and Proctor were on hand in 1949 to hear the premieres of Sonatina for Pianoforte and Quintet for Pianoforte and Strings.

For eight glorious years, Holmes wielded the baton. His term, like Gericke's with the BSO, introduced discipline to a slipshod ensemble and brought new, more powerful music to Boston audiences. An avid amateur photographer, he composed and arranged his orchestra by

113

Chadwick's old rule: he had an eye for its sound. His death—on Commencement Day, 1953—was an irreparable loss to the Conservatory. His last concert, in March, had demonstrated that. Racked by cancer, unable to stand for the performance, he nevertheless gave Jordan Hall at NEC audiences one last glimpse of his power, conducting a tender, haunting version of Fauré, followed by a stormy conclusion from Richard Strauss. Then, not yet forty-seven, he left Jordan Hall at NEC's stage.

Not, however, before introducing a new voice to the Conservatory. In September 1947 the Conservatory hired yet another choral director, a slight, scholarly, and dignified young educator whose work at Radcliffe and Bryn Mawr suggested that she might be up to the task where others, like Chadwick and Goodrich, had failed. Over the next forty-three years, Lorna Cooke deVaron created a nationally recognized chorus that, like Holmes's orchestra, balanced classical repertoire with exciting new pieces. She brought a unique sense of purpose and a formidable enthusiasm to her work. She was, as Holmes suspected, the kind of teacher who created choruses out of thin air and thin voices. She once concocted accompaniment by teaching the audience to sing along, though it consisted of delegates to the National Conference of Music Educators.

Lorna Cooke deVaron created a nationally recognized chorus that performed both classical and modern works.

On May 5, 1948, she led 150 singers of the New England Conservatory Chorus onto Jordan Hall stage. Over the next twenty years, she became a fixture there, conducting everything from the huge, massed voices of Honegger's *King David* to choral works by such modern artists as Vaughan Williams, Béla Bartók, and Aaron Copland, as well as Luigi Dallapiccola, her friend from the Berkshire Music Center, whose works the *Post* proclaimed as "highly original," but also "fiendishly difficult."

She joined Holmes in performances of Honegger and Schumann. She conducted the American debut of Handel's *Alexander Balus*, Conrad Beck's *Death over Basel*, and Schoenberg's notoriously difficult *Moses and Aron*, as well as a new work composed in 1962 by one of the Conservatory's own rising stars: Daniel Pinkham's *Easter Cantata*. And she turned her thoroughly drilled chorus over to a few trusted composers so that they might conduct their own works: Randall Thompson, for his *Frostiana*, and Fritz Büchtiger, for *John the Baptist*.

She also performed and recorded with the Boston Symphony Orchestra. Their joint interpretation of Berlioz's *Requiem* and Beethoven's Ninth Symphony won RCA Victor's award for best classical recording of 1959. And two years later, they won the National Academy of Recording Arts and Sciences's award for outstanding classical performance for their interpretation of Ravel's *Daphnis and Chloé*.

While the orchestra continued to grow in confidence and the chorus blossomed, opera faded into workshops and touring shows. It foundered on twin difficulties: Jordan Hall at NEC was too small and Boris Goldovsky was becoming too big for student productions. Goldovsky's 1946 *Figaro* was a rousing success but an obvious violation of the city's fire laws. That was nothing new—Goodrich had crowded Jordan's stage and exits for thirty years. But in the wake of the fateful Copacabana Club fire of 1944, Boston's officials and auditorium managers grew fearful. Even the Conservatory recognized the danger, bringing fireproof curtains and nonflammable seats into Jordan Hall at NEC.

Lorna Cooke de Varon and her students
during rehearsal.

So NEC opera had to find another
home. For the next eighteen years,
Goldovsky struggled to keep up his links
with Jordan Hall at NEC, relying on either
small works or modest orchestration to
overcome its limitations. On the one hand,
he presented such miniatures as Puccini's
Cloak, Menotti's *Old Maid and the Thief*,
Smetana's *Bartered Bride*, and Boston's first
performance of Strauss's *Ariadne auf Naxos*.
On the other, he presented "intimate"
stagings of larger works: a workshop version
of *The Magic Flute*, a *Faust* with only a
piano, Monteverdi's *L'Incoronazione di
Poppe*a—its first American performance—
with Goldovsky playing accompaniment on
a somewhat rusty harpsichord.

When the Metropolitan canceled its
Boston visit in 1947, he rushed his ever-
ready *Figaro* into action in the empty Opera
House and followed up his success with
La Bohème, Carmen, yet another *Figaro, Don
Giovanni, Eugene Onegin, Carmen* again,
and *Albert Herring*.

But his company—first named
the New England Opera Theater, then the
Goldovsky Opera Theater—neither filled
the hall nor paid the bills. The Conservatory
cut its subsidies. In 1957 the Opera House
closed. After almost five decades as a mon-
ument to Boston music, it was sold to
Northeastern University, razed, and turned
into a parking lot.

Goldovsky struggled on at Harvard's
Loeb Theater. There he staged his last
three Boston productions: New England
premieres of Carlisle Floyd's *Susannah*
and Robert Ward's *Crucible* and *The Turn
of the Screw*. They were fitting valedictories:
modern, idiomatic, and utterly American.
After their performances, however,
Goldovsky retired to the relative leisure
of his NEC visiting lectureship. The
Conservatory began to fret about opera
and "its need for improvement."

Goldovsky left a legacy of works
and also students who succeeded on larger
stages. Among the most notable were
Mildred Miller, who succeeded Eleanor
Steber as the Conservatory alumna
with the Metropolitan Opera; Jena Cox,
who sang at Bayreuth in the 1950s;
McHenry Boatwright, whose rich baritone
astounded American audiences;
and Sarah Caldwell, who joined Goldovsky
behind the curtain and took up his unhappy
struggle on behalf of Boston opera.

The orchestra, chorus, and opera were, as the trustees recognized, "our three most important public relations organizations." But they were only the most public successes of a school that was growing in prestige. New England Conservatory was becoming a recognized name in music in America and throughout the world. Tourjée, Chadwick, and Goodrich had sent out teachers; now their students made the long return voyage. NEC acknowledged the responsibilities that entailed and took on the task of educating young musicians from around the world. In 1946, Professor Z.Y. Wong, formerly at Yenching College, appealed for assistance on behalf of four talented musicians whose studies had been disrupted—and lives endangered—by China's raging civil war. The administration acted without hesitation: Wong and her charges were admitted, sight unseen and performances unheard. To satisfy the State Department's passport office, she was dubbed a visiting lecturer, and two of her group were awarded honorary scholarships.

That spontaneous act marked the beginning of a new era on Huntington Avenue. International students had arrived in earlier generations, drawn by the school's close ties to missionary movements and welcomed as curiosities. Now they came for professional education and were treated as fellow-citizens in a new musical world. By 1949, twenty-three of them had enrolled at the Conservatory; by 1966, thirty-five, the majority from Asia. Today, that trend continues, as more than a third of the school's musicians come from some thirty-three countries scattered around the world.

In those years, though, music needed all the help it could get. With East Asia reduced to poverty and war, Europe hungry and cold, and Latin America caught in a cycle of unrest and repression, music became a part of world politics. The State Department now dove into international student programs. So the Conservatory became an instrument in the orchestration of exchanges that, over the next forty-five years, gave new shape to the international musical community.

Musicians came from every corner of the world: Fulbright scholars from France, Institute of International Education students from Denmark, Rockefeller recipients from Colombia and Brazil, State Department-sponsored visitors from Korea and Japan. Conservatory students resumed their own studies abroad, though now they were as likely to go to Rome or Stockholm or Tokyo as their predecessors were to have gone to Munich or Paris. In 1951 the school began an exchange program with the Paris Conservatoire; a young French pianist came to study at NEC, and Sarah Lombardi, a Conservatory pianist and Fulbright scholar, continued her training in Paris. She was the first of a long line of Conservatory scholars. Over the next decade, graduates won more than twenty Fulbrights, as well as Beebe, Eames, and Rotary awards, for study abroad.

Wallace Goodrich (right) and Albert Schweitzer (left), who was made an honorary member of Pi Kappa Lambda in 1948.

The influx of international musicians changed the Conservatory. The narrow focus on European music began to broaden as students learned of other musical heritages. The Conservatory was becoming part of a world where music was a universal language. As it took its place in that world, it reached out to the masters of music. In September 1948, Pi Kappa Lambda made Albert Schweitzer an honorary member and, in fitting tribute, offered a recital of his organ music to benefit his African hospital. Two months later, Goldovsky welcomed Ernö Dohnányi, his old teacher and friend, to Huntington Avenue. An outstanding Hungarian conductor, composer, and champion of Kodály and Bartók, Dohnányi lectured and played in Jordan Hall at NEC. He also showed students that music in the modern world could not be insular: he defended Hungary's music but denounced its politics. He had raised his voice against its dictatorship in 1919, against the Fascist and anti-Semitic state that succeeded it in 1941, and against the Communist regime imposed in 1948. As a result, like many of his creative European colleagues, he spent most of his life in danger or in exile, an effective spokesman for music from a land that was no longer his own.

The next year, Conservatory students were treated to another kind of eloquence. In December 1949, Olivier Messiaen came to NEC to hear a performance of his *Quartet for the End of Time*. The piece employed unusual instrumentation: violin, cello, piano, and clarinet. Like any great composer, Messiaen molded his music to his circumstances. The Stalag VIII, a concentration camp near Görlitz where he had written it, had thrown out those instruments. So he had seized on them to make music and, in a personal cry of unsparing eloquence, defy his oppressors. The *Globe* critic found his work "dour and dissonant…intractable," but more modern audiences, educated to the horrors of the Holocaust, have heard in that dissonance a note of fierce personal integrity and even of hope.

In 1950 a young master of American music sauntered onto Jordan Hall stage. Aaron Copland regaled a crowded hall with stories about his compositions, less-than-flattering views of his contemporaries, and indecipherable ideas about his art. His homely conundrums and laughing asides poked fun at the growing complacency of a prosperous and powerful America. "In the old days," he reminded students, "artists looked like artists—with bow ties and long hair. Today artists look like businessmen. What a remarkable accomplishment."

That student conservatism lasted for a decade or more. In 1944, Quincy Porter reminded his trustees that a new generation of students was about to arrive: older, sobered by depression and war, shaped by army discipline. And increasingly they were men. Although women comprised 61 percent of students as late as 1954, men now took the greater number of degrees. Between 1947 and 1966, NEC awarded 1,054 baccalaureates, and more than half—595—went to men. In the preceding twenty years, they had received barely a third of them. And the master's degrees—increasingly becoming symbols of professional training—went to men as well. NEC awarded 483 between 1947 and 1966, 53.4 percent to men. There was, as the dean observed in 1962, "a certain regression in numbers and activity" among women in higher education.

This was, in Ruth McKay's phrase, "a marrying generation." As chair of the Conservatory's academic studies department (which Harrison Keller brought in for the teaching of literature and languages along university lines) and dean of students, she watched as talented women gave up career opportunities for more conventional and personal responsibilities. She had already begun to question the implications when she worked on the *Smith Alumnae Quarterly*, which had produced "If One Generation Can Ever Tell Another," the seed for Betty Friedan's ground-breaking *Feminine Mystique*. Male educators viewed the change more complacently. Explaining the decline in enrollments after the Korean War, the director blamed "interference from Uncle Sam or Cupid."

Coretta Scott studied voice and music education at the Conservatory in the early 1950s before marrying Martin Luther King, Jr., in 1953. Some years later, NEC awarded her an honorary doctorate of musical arts.

Cupid changed the ambitions, and ultimately the life, of one of the school's most distinguished graduates. In June 1953 a promising singer from Alabama married a Boston University graduate student. They remained in Boston for one more year, while the former Coretta Scott shifted from vocal performance to music education and her husband, Martin Luther King, Jr., worked on his dissertation. Then they returned to the South, taking up a cause that was to change the face and heart of America.

The Conservatory's embrace of African American students and music had been ambiguous. Tourjée had been raised in the abolitionist tradition. Chadwick, despite his affection for southerners, had welcomed black students. Henry Dunham and Wallace Goodrich had taught a generation of black church organists, singers, and educators. To celebrate the restoration of Jordan Hall at NEC in 1938, Goodrich had prevailed upon Roland Hayes to sing. By way of thanks, the school commemorated the hundredth anniversary of his birth in 1987. That was only part of the recognition of African American music that began with awards to Duke Ellington and Marian Anderson and continues today with festivals celebrating the place of African American music in America.

In 1872, Bostonians criticized the "primitive" songs of the Fisk Jubilee Singers, but NEC students rushed off to hear their rehearsals. In the wake of the Great War, young Americans had thrilled to jazz, while Conservatory teachers—including Chadwick—trained black students in the classical tradition. One of those students was William Grant Still, who recounted how he had arrived at NEC in 1923 to enroll. "As it happened, I was sent up to talk to Mr. Chadwick, who was director at the time, and he wanted to hear some of my things. When he heard them, he volunteered to teach me free of charge." Later

The career of renowned composer William Grant Still, whose musical style blended classical with rags, blues, and spirituals, got its start with Chadwick, who taught Still free of charge.

in his life, Still told an interviewer that African American students had been attracted to and accepted at Oberlin. He was asked: "Were there any other institutions at that time that had a reputation, that accepted Negroes and that had a good Music Department?" Still: "Yeah. The New England Conservatory." Interviewer: "The New England Conservatory?"

In the early 1950s, when the country awoke to the terrible implications of discrimination, NEC continued to take some pride in the many successes of its African American students. Among its distinguished graduates, besides Coretta Scott King, were Stanley Kirton, who went on to become an important educator; Raymond Jackson, the first African American to win the school's prestigious Chadwick Medal; Elwyn Adams, who worked as an index-card maker to pay his way to the 1955 International Music Festival—and became the first African American to win its competition. Annabelle Bernard became the second only two years later. As an outstanding classical vocalist, she toured Europe on behalf of the United States Information Service, where she was joined by Buckner Gamby, pianist and first of the school's African American Fulbright Scholars.

Probably the most popular of the school's African American vocalists, was McHenry Boatwright, who received a diploma in piano performance in 1950, then returned for a bachelor's degree in voice, which he earned in 1954. His debut in Jordan Hall at NEC, in February 1956, proved an auspicious beginning to a successful career: he sold out the hall, won over the critics, and brought the audience to its feet.

The Conservatory not only celebrated its minority artists but also gave thought to the "obstacles and difficulties" they had overcome. So when the Kennedy administration sent out a 1963 directive on "the civil rights problem," advising schools against discrimination, NEC trustees were, for a moment, at a loss. Finally they replied, with some asperity, that "there has never been a color bar in either the admissions or the placement policies of the Conservatory."

The Conservatory, though, had other problems. And they started at the top. For the first century, it had been guided by long-term directors and presidents: Tourjée had served for twenty-four years; Chadwick, for thirty-three; Goodrich, for twelve. Eben Jordan had presided over the board for eight years, the Browns for another twelve, and Philip Allen for sixteen. When two strong officers worked hand-in-hand—as Chadwick and Jordan, and later Goodrich and Allen, had—the Conservatory flourished. But a falling out, or a critical vacuum, led to difficulties.

In May 1946, Quincy Porter resigned. During the four war years, he had nursed the school through dwindling enrollment, a failing orchestra, and economic austerity. He had sacrificed his own work to the more practical concern of keeping his school afloat. By war's end, he had succeeded. So when Yale offered him its prestigious professorship of music, he accepted.

Boris Goldovsky (right) demonstrates a scene from Ariana Abandoned, *in which McHenry Boatwright (center) stars as Dionysos.*

President Allen promptly appointed Harrison Keller "acting" director, hardly a vote of confidence for a man who, like Goodrich before him, had dedicated his life to the school. After completing his education at Bethany College and serving in one of General Pershing's army bands, Keller had arrived at Huntington Avenue as a violin teacher in 1922. For twenty-four years, he worked with the school's lamentable string section and ensemble classes, led the Boston String Quartet, and filled in for the ailing Malcolm Holmes. His career, like Goodrich's, had focused on teaching, rather than performance. Like Goodrich, he was respected, rather than famous. At sixty-two, he was too loyal not to answer the call.

For the next twelve years, he presided over a Conservatory that faced new difficulties and new dangers. And he did so without Philip Allen. For the irascible, cane-wielding entrepreneur retired in December 1950, after serving the longest presidency in the school's history. More than any trustee since Jordan, he had sustained the Conservatory. As his friend John Macomber explained, he had found the place "absolutely busted financially and when I say busted, I mean busted." So he had borrowed and begged. Sixteen years later, he handed on a school that had retired its debt, burned its mortgage, turned a profit, and begun to consider expansion. He stepped down in favor of the younger, more energetic William T. Aldrich, but he continued to devote his failing days to one last legacy: an endowment.

After Holmes's death, Keller named Richard Burgin to conduct the NEC Orchestra. Like Keller, Burgin was a link to the school's past. He had served as the BSO concertmaster since 1920 and as associate conductor since 1932. Like Koussevitzky and Goldovsky, he had studied in Russia before the Revolution. At Petrograd Conservatory he first caught the modern sounds that he championed for the rest of his life. Burgin's most auspicious moment came in 1928, when he led the BSO Chamber Orchestra—and a perplexed audience—through Boston premieres of ome of the great works of modern music: Louis Gruenberg's *Daniel Jazz*, Hindemith's *Marienleben*, Schoenberg's *Pierrot Lunaire*, and Stravinsky's Octet. In 1943 he steered the BSO through its first performance of two more modern works: Vladimir Dukelsky's Violin Concerto and George Gershwin's *Porgy and Bess*. Now sixty-five, Burgin was, like Keller, the aging occupant of a demanding job. Like Keller, he took up the work out of a love for the school. And like Keller, he was pushed aside when trouble returned to Huntington Avenue.

Keller's ambition was to educate "even better performers, intelligent citizens, and responsible future leaders." In 1952 he recast the Conservatory as "a college of music," taking the title of president and designating Aldrich chairman of the Board of Trustees. In addition to establishing the academic studies departments, he strengthened the school's classroom instruction, developed a four-year theory program rooted in "live musical experience." He envisioned a "magic number" of five to six hundred students, including a hundred candidates for the master's degree.

Former BSO concertmaster and associate conductor Richard Burgin was conductor of the NEC Orchestra during Keller's reign.

*Former violin faculty member Harrison
Keller took the reins from Quincy Porter when
he retired in 1946.*

He ruthlessly weeded out the old
diploma, a certificate that blighted his idea
of a musical college. Instead, he created the
new Artist Diploma in 1946, awarded to
especially gifted performers, those he considered "the potential orchids of the
Conservatory." The first of his flowers was
flutist Lois Schaefer, who received the
new award in 1947 and then blossomed
with the BSO.

In 1950 he introduced instruction
for musicians aged five to eighteen in
"the most modern methods." Modeled on
programs at Eastman and Juilliard, his
Department of Music for Young People
bloomed almost overnight, enrolling
eighty-five students in its first year. So he
campaigned for an independent preparatory school, outside the hothouse of
Huntington Avenue, where teachers could
encourage young talent, the basis for
later NEC preparatory school programs
scattered across Boston's suburbs.

He also petitioned Massachusetts
for the right to confer honorary degrees,
then awarded his school's first honorary
doctorate of musical arts in 1956 to Howard
Hanson, an outstanding American
composer and dean of the Eastman School,
NEC's primary rival. Over the next forty
years, NEC conferred honorary degrees as a
way of thanking its friends, celebrating
its teachers, and recognizing greatness in
both music and the wider world. The
school honored Boris Goldovsky, Nadia
Boulanger, and Eleanor Steber. It honored
Carl McKinley, Richard Burgin, and
Lorna Cooke deVaron. And it celebrated not
only Elliott Carter, Aaron Copland, and
Beverly Sills, but Marian Anderson, Senator
Claiborne Pell, Herbert Marcuse, and
Coretta Scott King. Today, the recipients
continue to remind graduating students
of the Conservatory's commitment to producing not only better musicians but, as
Keller had hoped, more responsible citizens.

Keller's mission and style rubbed
off on his students. While trustees longed for
some "great man" to lead the Conservatory,
their president made it a more relaxed place
to work and live. In keeping with his commitment to educating citizens, he brought
in national figures to give students a taste
of music and theater as well as politics.
He also gave the drama classes an opportunity to perform on the Jordan Hall stage.
In 1947, a capacity audience watched as the
stately hall was transformed into an
idyllic New England village for Thornton
Wilder's *Our Town*.

He also introduced one of the Conservatory's most informal and fondly remembered events. With assistance from Holmes (clad in what one onlooker called "a rather spectacular version of a sweatshirt"), he staged an evening of informal sight-readings of major pieces such as Brahms's *Requiem* in Jordan Hall at NEC. In a school where competition and professionalism were already the norms, he urged people to drop by, pick up scores, and try their collective hand. Students, teachers, administrators, and a few strays took him up on his offer. Jordan Hall at NEC once again echoed to the enthusiasm that brought them all together and to the amateurism they were leaving behind. The performance was sloppy, exhilarating, and carried off with no stars and no audience. It was, as Keller reminded his young charges, "for fun only."

Keller brought fun, as well as learning, to Jordan Hall at NEC. Even Dohnányi ended his slightly formal appearance in a rollicking piano duet with Goldovsky. Copland, who never even feigned formality, told jokes, played tunes, and beguiled his audience. Less notable performers also brought their talents. The Program of Popular Music played some jazz, while the Conservatory Band entertained more sedate audiences with a brass repertoire already sliding into history. From the more distant past, musical historian Warren Storey Smith introduced Irish songs to students who barely knew a ballad from a jig. Smith and his wife spent their lives collecting, transcribing, and so preserving thousands of Irish folk songs. In keeping with his commitment to making music come to life, Keller persuaded the Smiths to perform their old songs in Jordan Hall at NEC, where they were accompanied by an extremely talented young pianist, John Moriarty.

Had NEC flourished, Keller might have been remembered for his enthusiasm, love of music, and sense of fun. But it fell to him to face another of the Conservatory's crises, and he failed that last, harsh test. For the good times were drawing to a close. By 1951 the last of the veterans had graduated, and the Korean War reduced student ranks. A small cloud appeared on the horizon: enrollment fell by 20 percent, and the treasurer reported that, after allowing for depreciation, the school sustained its first loss since 1945.

Small, but manageable losses became routine. The school went into the red in four of the next five years, accumulating deficits of $140,000. Enrollment continued to fall or was driven down by Keller's effort to create a small, professional school for gifted musicians. And though the preparatory and graduate programs flourished, they were not yet able to sustain the school's reputation or its budget.

Boston was changing. Although the Huntington Avenue trolley had mercifully gone underground, the city had not yet spread west. The Opera House was on the verge of being torn down. Railroad lines, decaying homes, and declining businesses combined to produce the worst environment for a school: a neighborhood that was dreary, out of the way, and unsafe.

The Conservatory seemed headed that way as well. Its dormitories had been taken out of mothballs during the war, and the musty odor of disuse clung to their small rooms and dark stairwells.

They were dilapidated and distant. Built to house young women, they were now so far away that school officers feared for the students' safety. Trustees warned that Huntington Avenue was becoming another Franklin Square, and they urged that the school take refuge in more genteel suburbs, perhaps in bucolic Brookline. They even considered taking Jordan Hall at NEC and Beethoven along with them as mementos of fifty years' work.

Keller and his new dean, Chester Williams, did what they could. They campaigned for more scholarships, increased government assistance, and better faculties to make their professional school preeminent. And they threw themselves into increasing enrollment. They failed, but their efforts did much to slow the ebbing tide.

Others noticed the Conservatory's decline. In 1955, in response to Keller's appeal for funding, the Rockefeller Foundation refused to support an orchestral study program on the grounds that the idea was neither new nor educationally ambitious. The Ford Foundation, meanwhile, showed cautious faith, agreeing to provide $132,600 "for the purpose of increasing faculty salaries." In ten years, the Conservatory had lost its stature and its vision. To the outside world, it was just becoming another needy school.

The solution, Keller insisted, was to rebuild. He led the campaign to sell off old buildings, buy up adjacent property, and build a new dormitory and library. The trustees were divided, but they agreed to support Keller. He had already won not only the Ford Foundation grant but also awards of $200,000 from Mrs. Rockefeller and $175,000 from the Harriet Spaulding Charitable Trust. He had also secured a $1.4 million government building loan on very

easy terms. He even shrank the deficits. Keller's strategy of rebuilding struck the trustees as the only alternative to austerity.

Already seventy, Keller was not up to the task of rebuilding the Conservatory. In September 1957 he retired, and the trustees began their search for "a great man" to succeed him. The new president faced a critical challenge: by 1957 enrollment had fallen to only 410 students; the deficit had shot back up to $30,000. But there were grounds for hope: the government loan had gone through. Northeastern had offered $200,000 for the old dorms, and a fund drive had raised more than $600,000. For the pessimists, the financial glass was half-full and leaking. For the optimists, there was plenty more where that came from.

In February 1958 the trustees unanimously elected Dr. James Aliferis as their seventh director, or second president. Not yet forty-five, he presented impressive credentials for the job. After studying at Western Reserve with that longtime Conservatory friend, Arthur Shepherd, he taught at the University of Minnesota, where he developed a standardized evaluation form, the Aliferis Music Achievement Test. More than a pedagogue, at Minnesota he had conducted the University Chorus and, on occasion, took the baton from his friend Dmitri Mitropoulos—who, as Aliferis inevitably reminded people, "had discovered Leonard Bernstein."

Aliferis came to Huntington Avenue with an ambitious program, handpicked assistants, and unanimous support from the trustees. He began with the faculty. He took up Keller's effort to provide pensions, securing a contributory program that continues to this day. He weeded out many of the school's part-timers, replacing them with a small circle of full-time, academically distinguished professionals. Then he changed the curriculum. In keeping with his ideal of a college, he drew up what he called a "core curriculum" for his students, which required a year's study in fine arts, two years in literature, and two in language. Those were to be taught in large lecture classes by "master teachers," with graduate students supervising smaller "drill

Dorm and library from Huntington Avenue

sections." To attract those students, he urged the Conservatory to prepare yet another degree program, the doctor of musical arts. Because the D.M.A. wasn't essential for a teaching career, the idea was shelved. (The Conservatory finally established a D.M.A. program in 1992.)

He offered an ambitious vision of the Conservatory's future, propped up by the charts and graphs that delighted him. But the vision was also perilous, for Aliferis saw the Conservatory as a miniature version of a huge state school, where students were to be regimented and trained in large groups, rather than in the intimate classes that had made the place special. Aliferis broke ground for the new dormitory. Construction began slowly and proceeded expensively. The building provided a library, cafeteria, and accommodations for 168 students. The original plan had been to house only women, so architects had designed "special hairwashing equipment…a make-up counter…and storage cubicles for cosmetics." But Aliferis convinced the trustees to allocate two floors to men. So when the dormitory finally opened in the fall of

1960, the cosmetic counters and hair dryers were gone, displaced by the new venture of co-educational living.

The main building, though noble in contrast to the new dormitory's inhospitable, institutional aesthetic, had come on hard times. The years of neglect and forced economies began to tell. It was shabby, in need of repair or replacement. Aliferis discovered, for example, that the building's electricity was still generated in-house, using steam diverted from a Con Edison pipe under Huntington Avenue. That had been state-of-the-art in 1902, but it was now utterly obsolete: it produced direct current, which blew out the school's equipment. So Aliferis convinced the trustees to spend the money to hook the Conservatory to a contemporary supply of alternating current.

Aliferis had more plans. He reinvented the music theory program, bringing in an expert to teach a new, required class in eurhythmics. Forty years earlier, Chadwick had dabbled with Dalcroze's ideas as a way of encouraging individual understanding. Aliferis, fortified by his work on standardized tests for large schools, now decided to make eurhythmics part of his curriculum.

Other changes followed. The Popular Music Department disappeared. Music therapy, first offered as part of a new idea in music education, followed. In their place, Aliferis, imitating Juilliard, resurrected dance. Esther Brooks, a prominent local dancer, and Robert Cohan, once a partner to Martha Graham, installed a barre in Brown Hall, trained a handful of students, and lobbied for the use of Jordan Hall at NEC.

The new president had a fondness for charts and tables, but he was occasionally clumsy with people. In 1959 he hired James Dixon, another of Mitropoulos's "discoveries," to conduct the orchestra. In a brusque move he also announced that Burgin was therefore relieved of his duties as conductor and was to have his salary reduced accordingly. It was an unnecessary slight to a man who, now in failing health, had done his best for the Conservatory. Then, with a minimum of discussion, he disbanded the Boston String Quartet. The move made sense: the Quartet now rarely performed and, with Keller's retirement, had lost most of its energy. But it was, again, a blow to the music, and the people, that made NEC unique.

The same clumsiness appeared two years later, when Lorna Cooke deVaron requested a sabbatical. For fourteen years, she had taught and conducted, filling her few free moments with tours, recordings, and the search for new music. She

had made the chorus a permanent and distinguished part of Conservatory life, a task that had defeated even Chadwick. Now she asked for a rest, and Aliferis refused. Sabbaticals were not in his budget or his master plan. So he offered her a year's leave of absence, unpaid. That saved money, but embarrassed both the teacher and the school.

Aliferis did as badly with Dr. Maurice Fremont-Smith. The new chairman never warmed to Aliferis. The two found themselves increasingly at odds over the curriculum, the faculty, and the place of the Conservatory. So in April 1960, Fremont-Smith abruptly resigned, despite pleas from fellow trustees. He was succeeded by Sherwin Badger, vice-president of New England Mutual and a shrewder judge of character. He and Aliferis didn't get on much better, feuding about costs, faculty unrest, and Aliferis's management style.

Idabelle Firestone, for whom NEC's music library is named. Created in 1928, "The Voice of Firestone" was one of the country's first radio programs before it moved on to television in 1949. The award-winning show featured world-renowned opera stars such as Risë Stevens, Richard Tucker, Franco Corelli, Renata Tebaldi, Leontyne Price, and NEC alumna Eleanor Steber, who appeared on the program thirty-six times, as well as artists such as Rudolph Nureyev, Rosemary Clooney, Chita Rivera, and Jacques d'Amboise.

The valuable Voice of Firestone collection wound up at New England Conservatory thanks to Harvey Phillips, an executive assistant at NEC and a well-known tuba player, and his friend, Harvey S. Firestone, Jr., CEO of Firestone Tire & Rubber Company. Firestone, whose mother Idabelle composed the show's theme song, turned to the Conservatory for a safe place to store the 485 kinescopes and 43 master tapes of the television and radio programs.

The Conservatory, nevertheless, was a place to make music. And it did. In 1959, Dmitri Shostakovich visited as part of a Soviet musical delegation, the beginning of NEC's long, amicable tie with Russian musicians. When the chorus sang Bach's *Alleluia* in his honor, the composer was moved to tears. Three months later, he returned the favor. As part of a concert to raise scholarship funds, James Dixon stepped onto the Jordan Hall stage and conducted the Boston premiere of Shostakovich's Tenth Symphony—a grand testimony to the genius hidden behind that silence. The remainder of the program was almost as impressive: Jesús Sanromá, one of the school's most generous graduates, performed a Mozart Concerto, and Walter Piston conducted his own Concertino.

Aliferis encouraged those kinds of performances, which made the Conservatory an exciting place for students and their teachers: in 1959 he found the time and money to launch a series of annual festivals that have more than repaid their debt over the years. The highlight of the first was the local debut of Floyd's *Susannah*; of the second, the first Boston performance of Mahler's Third Symphony. In 1961 the orchestra performed for the Music Educators' National Conference in Washington. It was an impressive tribute to its growing stature, though Aliferis fretted over how to pay for the travel.

Money was becoming critical. Each year Aliferis presented charts and calculations proving that he had turned the Conservatory around, and each year it sank further into debt. In his last year, Keller had lost $30,000. Aliferis predicted a smaller loss, then reported one of $40,000 before

finally admitting that he had sustained the worst deficit in the school's postwar history: $63,000. That was to be the pattern for Aliferis's financial reports: rosy predictions, followed by mild warnings, ending in catastrophic losses. His optimistic but unreliable calculations not only undercut efforts at economy but reduced the school's precious reserves. For the trustees agreed to ease their new president's task by covering small deficits out of the carefully nurtured reserve and unrestricted funds. Now those payments were becoming part of his debt-ridden routine.

The deficits grew. Aliferis predicted a loss of $40,000 in 1958–59, then reported one of $85,000. The next year, he offered a prediction of stunning precision: the school would lose $39,498. Six months later, he changed that to $60,000, before finally admitting he had lost $141,000. His efforts infuriated the trustees: each year he predicted improvement; each year the books got worse.

The trustees watched in confusion and horror as their reserve fund drained away. By 1962 it had fallen from $526,000 to $354,000, and the trustees did not expect matters to improve. Badger had had enough. The problem, he insisted, was not "cost control," but enrollment. Aliferis's cheerful prognostications never quite translated into registrations. The new dormitory, with forty empty beds, was losing money. The expensive new courses had too few students. So Aliferis, who had offered to resign when Badger first took the chair, did so again. This time the trustees accepted. He had lasted less than four years.

They named Chester Williams their new president. Like Goodrich and Keller, he was a Conservatory veteran. For the past sixteen years, he had taught music theory and served as executive dean of the Conservatory and dean of graduate students. In a school that Aliferis had stocked with supporters, he represented the old guard. His loyalty was neither to the beleaguered president nor the irate trustees, but to the Conservatory and its students. For them, he had all but given up his oboe and spent months on the road, scouting new students and publicizing his school.

Williams now took a difficult office, burdened by three tasks. He had to staunch the flow of red ink. He had to find students. And he had to dismantle Aliferis's lockstep curriculum. He recognized that under Aliferis the Conservatory had veered off in the direction of universities, so he began by reclaiming the school's original mission: "To produce good performers and good teachers…We should not engage in teaching and musicology," he told trustees. "Harvard can and will always make a better job of it."

He took a symbolic step at commencement. There he introduced graduates and parents to his first guest speaker and degree recipient: Isaac Stern. And, by way of apology, he awarded another degree to a more familiar face: Richard Burgin. Williams wanted to stress music, so he dismantled Aliferis's curriculum, reduced the number of course offerings, and shifted some of the class work to Simmons College. His school was a conservatory, so he focused on music.

Badger and Williams revived the idea of a string quartet, restored master classes, and rejuvenated the orchestra. Under Aliferis, the Boston String Quartet had disappeared. Williams now persuaded Joseph Silverstein, George Zazofsky, Joseph de Pasquale, and Samuel Mayes to take up residence as the Nova Arte Quartet, to give three Jordan Hall at NEC performances, and to play for WGBH radio.

He then appointed Frederick Prausnitz as orchestra conductor. For the next five years, this fiery champion of modern music insisted on at least one new piece for each concert. For the first time, Jordan Hall at NEC audiences heard such works as William Schuman's *New England Triptych*, George Rochberg's *Night Music*, Peter Mennin's Sixth Symphony, Roger Sessions's Fourth Symphony, and Karl Hartmann's Second Symphony, as well as Daniel Pinkham's *Catacoustical Measures*.

Williams even welcomed the eccentricities of electronic music, giving premieres of works by Karlheinz Stockhausen and inviting Edgar Varèse to a performance of his *Deserts*, a work for orchestra, forty-nine percussion instruments, and tape machine. It was a tribute to the orchestra, or to the composer's good sense, that Varèse graciously declined to conduct, play, or beat on any of those drums. He did agree to turn on the tape. Prausnitz educated his young musicians and audiences in the troubling idiom of contemporary music. He joined with Cooke deVaron to present an homage to contemporary Italian composers, the first American production of Bruckner's Third Symphony in more than sixty years, and the national premiere of Beck's *Death over Basel*.

The chorus, too, summoned new energies and marched on. Cooke deVaron convinced first Randall Thompson and then Fritz Büchtiger to conduct their works in Jordan Hall at NEC. She debuted Beck's difficult piece and then, in a still more difficult performance, joined the BSO in Leonard Bernstein's *Kaddish*, a sad tribute to the late John F. Kennedy. Her status as educator and artist received public recognition in 1966, when the State Department asked her chorus to tour the Soviet Union, the second link between the Conservatory and the Russian music world.

Even the opera department played a new, though less dramatic, role. Goldovsky continued to serve as a "visiting lecturer," but Williams entrusted his opera program to Thomas Phillips and Ross Reimueller, former stage and musical directors to the impresario. They combined to produce Menotti's *Medium* and Puccini's *Cloak in Brown Hall*, followed by Menotti's *Saint of Bleecker Street* and then *Hänsel und Gretel*, and concluded their tenure with a Jordan Hall at NEC production of *Figaro* in February 1966. Then the Conservatory, plagued by the lack of money and a stage, once again gave up on opera.

Williams was forced to cut back on every front. He dumped eurhythmics as quickly as he could. When the dance troupe demanded more money and the use of Jordan Hall at NEC, he got rid of the entire program. Commissioned by the trustees to hire faculty with "the highest reputation as musicians," he searched out promising talent instead. New, young teachers like Robert Ceely brought different, challenging sounds to their students. In preparing for its hundredth anniversary, the Conservatory paid tribute to its composition department: Robert Cogan, along with Walter Piston, produced orchestral pieces; Daniel Pinkham joined Randall Thompson in composing choral works.

NEC students (in blazers) pose with Moscow Conservatory students during the Chorus's 1966 trip to the Soviet Union.

Talent seemed to have taken refuge on Huntington Avenue. Cooke deVaron's renown spread as awards accumulated and touring invitations poured in. Pinkham's works were performed by Bernstein and his New York Philharmonic Orchestra. And in what was at least a tribute to his energy, William Tesson finished *The Harmonic Idiom of the Jazz Orchestra* while busy conducting his own, slightly less prestigious ensemble—the Mickey Rooney Las Vegas Review.

Williams championed one last musical cause. He orchestrated the Castle Hill Summer Program, which brought gifted students and remarkable teachers to the beautiful mansion overlooking Crane's Beach in Ipswich. Among the guests he lured to that quiet summer retreat were Boris Goldovsky, the Esterhazy Orchestra, Peter Serkin, and Itzhak Perlman. The eight-week program was not a financial success, but even the trustees, desperate for economies, agreed that they had to keep it going.

Nevertheless, financial worries continued to plague them. Enrollments fell: in 1960, NEC had registered 114 freshmen; in 1961, 87; in 1962, only 72. By 1963, the school had a mere 236 undergraduates and was in danger of disappearing. Registration began to bounce back in 1963. Williams even managed—for the first time—to fill the dormitory. But deficits followed the decline. For Williams was never able to break the pattern of losses that he inherited. In three years, NEC accumulated debts of $425,000. Then in March 1966, his treasurer announced terrifying news: he and Williams anticipated a deficit of $360,000, more than twice the size of any previous losses.

The Conservatory was on the brink of ruin, with only one straw left to grasp. Eight months earlier, Mrs. Rockefeller had again made a generous contribution, offering up to $1 million in assistance, provided that the school could raise matching funds of another $3 million. Philip Allen's old dream of an endowment drive now had to be undertaken, or the school would have to close. For that, the Conservatory needed a charismatic "great man" to wring money from the musical community, the foundations, and the public.

Williams knew that, as much as he loved the school, he was not the man for the job. So eleven days after the fateful treasurer's report, he resigned, citing "the changing demands of the presidency." He had stabilized the school's reputation and its music, but now he had to step aside, hoping that some better-known leader could raise the money. That, he knew, was the only way the school could survive. As he told the trustees, "In this we must succeed."

A postcard of New England Conservatory

The New England Conservatory
Ragtime Ensemble
CONDUCTED BY
Gunther Schuller

GUNTHER SCHULLER: THE COMPLETE MUSICIAN

9

Retain of the past only that which you may need in the future.

—*Mark Twain*

In its first century, New England Conservatory had gone from obscurity to international renown. Tourjée had shaped his school to the market and his own vision. Chadwick had forged an American College of Music. Their successes had strengthened, expanded, and established the Conservatory's place in the musical world. So, in 1967, the trustees prepared for the Conservatory's second century; they named Gunther Schuller as the school's president. In doing so, they began a new mission, led by a visionary who was to reshape the Conservatory. Under Schuller, NEC leapt to the forefront of music. Yet even as it grew into its new role and music, it was threatened by an old nemesis: financial insecurity.

Schuller brought a personal and musical presence that the Conservatory had not had since Chadwick. As the son of a New York Philharmonic violinist, he had

begun composing and playing the French horn at an early age. At eighteen, he was already the principal horn in the Cincinnati Symphony; at twenty, principal in the Metropolitan Opera Orchestra. He not only composed, wrote, broadcast, and conducted but also taught at the Manhattan and Yale schools of music. A self-taught composer, he produced an extraordinary range of work, drawing on contemporary music, jazz, and improvisation. And on the eve of his arrival in Boston, his first opera, *The Visitation*, premiered in Vienna.

Schuller's professional life and his abilities as an autodidact shaped his thinking both about music and the training of musicians. Like Chadwick, he was a driven man, determined to realize the highest standards. With his prodigious energy and modern ambitions, he planned to transform a tranquil institution into a leader in musical and social change.

Schuller moved quickly. Even before taking office, he spoke of the challenges facing the Conservatory and of his vision for meeting them. He noted that the school's "conservative, tradition-perpetuating function" posed difficult problems in a society where vast social, economic, and cultural changes had precipitated "an esthetic tug-of-war" between secure defenders of the past and prophets of a transfigured future. The Conservatory had to infuse a new spirit into its tradition, "lest it become merely a museum."

For Schuller, the choice was simple: "Does the Conservatory take the lead in the musical community, or does it passively supply a demand determined by performing organizations, or does it defer the whole problem to the experimental centers at the universities?" His answer was to make his new school a leader in American musical education.

He did so by expanding the dimensions of the Conservatory and re-evaluating the place of the old and the new. He focused on his vision of the "total musician" and the "complete Conservatory." By the former, he meant someone who aspired to both intellectual and emotional realization. In an age when music had become a highly specialized profession driven by

Gunther Schuller's Ragtime Ensemble was just one of the many new changes he brought to the Conservatory.

a narrow repertoire, he insisted that his Conservatory develop musicians with personal visions of their art. He scorned music as business. He wanted a "vehicle for expressing feelings, thoughts, ideas—those of the composer he is performing and even (if he has earned the privilege) those of himself." And he planned to educate this complete musician by creating a "complete Conservatory." Such a school had not only a depth of musical forces but a breadth of vision, one in which "the many subsidiary disciplines, whether applied or theoretical, whether individual or collective, are all integrated, aware of each other, enlightened by each other."

Schuller's mission posed the most dramatic challenge to the school since Chadwick's era. It had essentially remained as Chadwick had left it, unaffected by changes in the musical economy, in technology, or in contemporary music. Schuller, with typical gusto, served notice that change was coming, and the institution braced for what was to follow.

Faculty were apprehensive about their place in Schuller's new order. He reassured them by asking the popular Chester Williams, his predecessor, to stay on as dean, but he invested new powers in two assistants, Donald Harris and Harvey Phillips. With their help, Schuller interceded in every aspect of the institution: he argued, he persuaded, he intimidated. His drive and magnetism brought reform to the school, but at a price.

From his first days, as the trustees noted, the place was "bristling with activity and a new sense of direction." That became even clearer during the new president's inauguration. The celebration, tied to NEC's centennial, included a symposium on "The Conservatory Redefined." Distinguished speakers addressed a century of changes in music, technology, and research, then speculated about the next hundred years. Even as the Conservatory celebrated its past, Schuller was at work shaping the future.

While Schuller planned, however, Conservatory deficits continued to grow. In February 1967 the trustees' treasurer reported that past budgets had "been knowingly exceeded on the theory that improved quality would create the capacity to raise the needed money." That perilous strategy now endangered the school. Schuller had to not only recreate the Conservatory but accomplish his work with few resources, fitful community support, and a hearty dose of bad luck.

In his inaugural speech, Schuller pledged to eliminate degrees that Chadwick had labored to create. For almost half a century, they had testified to the school's legitimacy. For Schuller, they symbolized authority and regimentation. As a first step, he abandoned grades, even as he raised the standards of admission. The result was a school that both insisted on and repudiated standards, that conserved and experimented, that looked to the past and rushed into the future. Dean Chester Williams, in the thick of those changes, noted, "The curriculum was in a constant state of flux."

Schuller's new curriculum featured a new program in early music performance, a revamped music education program committed to developing "an elite of music educators who will be Musicians first and Educators second," and a revitalized composition department to resume its place at the core of the Conservatory as the "heart and soul of music." Schuller also recast the school's humanities program to focus on the musicians' role in contemporary society. He developed the same themes in formal weekly assemblies where artists and performers shared their insights with students. The Stan Kenton Orchestra, Professor Ramanathan of India, the French National Radio Orchestra, and the composer Luigi Dallapiccola all appeared to discuss everything from jazz composition to new woodwind techniques. And the president transformed the Conservatory Symphony and Repertory orchestras' repertoire to feature more contemporary music.

Perhaps nothing exemplified Schuller's philosophy so well as that repertoire. Like Chadwick before him, Schuller combined the role of president with that of composer and conductor, determined to achieve masterful performance of contemporary music. And yet, like Chadwick, he insisted on systematic training in traditional works. His first three programs reflected his paradoxical ambitions. He began his career in Jordan Hall at NEC on October 19, 1967, by inviting Dallapiccola to conduct Mozart's *Haffner Symphony*, Ravel's *Bolero*, and four of his own songs. For NEC's centennial concert on November 15, he asked Randall Thompson to lead the orchestra through both Mahler's First Symphony and his own *Psalm of Thanksgiving*, a work commissioned in honor of Maurice Fremont-Smith, the Conservatory's former chairman. Schuller first conducted his orchestra at the Christmas concert on December 13, with Lorna Cooke deVaron leading her chorus in Russian liturgical motets and twentieth-century English carols, followed by a performance of his own *Psalm XCVIII, A Sacred Cantata*, and Robert Cogan's *whirl…ds (1)*. It was the Boston premiere of his work, and the world premiere of Cogan's.

Schuller went on to conduct works by Yun, Weill, Busoni, Reznicek, Gerhard, Peyton, Serocki, Converse, Schoenberg, Sibelius, Stravinsky, Sessions, Goehr, Webern, Piston, Debussy, Berg, Copland, Bernstein, Becker, and Martino along with those of Brahms, Mozart, Beethoven, Strauss, and Berlioz. The orchestra echoed Schuller's interest in contemporary music, offering programs that, two decades later, were still regarded with pride and even awe. In the school's 1969 festival, it offered a program of Stravinsky's music that included *Three Anthems, Symphony of Psalms*, and *Les Noces*, all played before a packed, hushed, and appreciative audience.

With his credentials in contemporary music, Schuller looked farther ahead. In June 1969, he stunned the quiet world of music educators. As of September, the Conservatory would offer a program— the country's first at a classical conservatory —in jazz. Like Chadwick, Schuller hoped to encourage American music, and he saw in jazz a major contribution to the music of the world. So he launched a full-fledged program in jazz performance, jazz history, and jazz theory. To reassure wary applicants, he warned that "requirements in this degree program are stringent."

Chester Williams confessed that the venture took the form of a "kidnapping." Schuller swooped down on Berklee College of Music, scooped up its best performers, and hired them to lead the new "Jazz Studies." But Schuller did not simply move a jazz program down the street. He focused on his erudition and enthusiasm for the form's theory and history, its connections to music, and most important, its defining disciplines of arrangement and improvisation. He named Carl Atkins head of the department and appointed George Russell,

Sensing that the times were changing, Gunther Schuller brought a new mission to the Conservatory in 1967, introducing jazz, Third Stream, early music, and Community Services, and revamping music education.

an internationally recognized composer and pianist, to the faculty. The department has since attracted such important artists to the faculty as Jaki Byard, Ernie Wilkins, Thad Jones, Barry Galbraith, Miroslav Vitous, Phil Wilson, Joe Allard, Dave Holland, Stanley Cowell, Jimmy Giuffre, Bob Moses, and William Thomas McKinley, while welcoming such guest teachers as Dizzy Gillespie, Gil Evans, Anthony Braxton, Bob Brookmeyer, Randy Weston, and Gerald Wilson.

To recruit students for his new program, Schuller traveled around the country, visiting hundreds of schools and jazz ensembles. In Philadelphia he spoke to a young man looking for a place to study jazz. Schuller convinced him that jazz enjoyed a prominent place in NEC's musical curriculum. Fifteen years later that prospective student, Hankus Netsky, became chairman of the Jazz Department and formed the Klezmer Conservatory Band, an internationally acclaimed Yiddish music group.

By adding jazz to his curriculum, Schuller broke with the tradition of the Conservatory as a museum, preserving the works of its European ancestors. NEC had become instead a festival, incorporating the rich, colorful panorama of contemporary musics. Over the next quarter of a century, jazz flourished. Today it attracts a tenth of the Conservatory's students. As in the days of Chadwick, the school again led the way in musical education, forcing other places to follow in its wake.

Jazz, though, was only one step. Schuller wanted his Conservatory to leap out of its traditionalism and welcome the changed society in which new music grew. He wanted to reach out to the African American community, to engage the neighborhoods of Roxbury in a constant dialogue on music, performance, education, and culture.

African American students had been welcomed at the Conservatory since the time of Tourjée, but they had been invited to study European music and techniques. Chadwick had continued that tradition, narrowed by his own genteel sensibility. But in the midst of America's struggle for civil rights, the Conservatory recognized that it had to do more.

It began by providing "socially conscious students" opportunities to teach and perform in the community and so created NEC's commitment to community services. Conservatory faculty taught in the Elma Lewis School of Fine Arts in Roxbury, young musicians studied at the Conservatory, and orchestral players volunteered to coach minority performers. A program for working within the prison system, funded by the Ford Foundation, drew praise from legislators, prison officials, and the national media. The Conservatory's Community Services Department grew to forty teachers and 185 students, ranging from thirteen to nineteen years old.

The Klezmer Conservatory Band, created by Jazz Studies Chairman Hankus Netsky (kneeling, left), performed Yiddish music.

To support that effort, NEC launched its "New Generation" program, in which the chorus and orchestra worked closely with Boston's most impoverished public schools to teach music and educate its own students in wider social concerns. Community Services joined hands with the Extension Division on October 28, 1972, for Jordan Hall at NEC's grand Mardi Gras Festival. For a rare moment, racially troubled Boston listened while its students offered the music that thrived in its clashing cultures. Schuller vigorously supported his vision of community service, though it drained away precious resources. As the school's finances came to a crisis, though, he was forced to sacrifice that vision to insure the school's survival. His hopes of forging links between the Conservatory and its neighbors withered in the face of financial difficulties: foundations grew wary, and the government became absorbed in its own tragedy in Vietnam. Schuller never lost sight of his ambition, however. To remind both his neighbors and his school of music's place in the culture, he invited one of NEC's most famous graduates to speak at commencement and receive an honorary degree. Coretta Scott King, who had taken her undergraduate degree in 1954, returned in 1971 to survey the changes Schuller had made and to inspire a new generation of NEC graduates.

Other changes to the Conservatory continued. Schuller transformed his faculty, squeezing out the old guard and introducing new, exciting teachers. The transformation had the speed and severity of a purge. But the new faculty made a difference. Schuller made a series of appointments to the String Department that formed its nucleus: Eric Rosenblith, Scott Nickrenz, Laurence Lesser, and Masuko Ushioda. Other artists added their talents and energy to other departments, notably, Russell Sherman, new chairman of the piano department; Ran Blake, Community Services (and later Third Stream) chairman; John Heiss, the flutist and composer who championed twentieth-century music into the curriculum; and Donald Martino, whose works won a Pulitzer Prize. Others included Veronica Jochum, Frank Battisti, Wya-Kyung Byun, Gabriel Chodos, Robert DiDomenica, Patricia Zander, and Benjamin Zander.

Schuller next turned his ear to world music. The walls of music were breaking down. He was determined to lead the way. He hired Peter Row to teach Indian music, even investing his own money to buy the necessary sitars. He also developed what he had called "third stream" music, a "synthesis of various creative tendencies, including jazz and contemporary European influences." The elements for that were already in place. Now Schuller tried to construct a sophisticated language out of the "happy marriage between jazz and non-jazz." In his own works, he carefully explored that fusion: he wrote *Transformation* as an evolution from the modern twelve-tone into jazz and back again. He set a jazz band against a string quartet and symphony orchestra. His *Seven Studies on Themes by Paul Klee*, First Symphony, and *Visitation* moved still closer to a synthesis of modern classical music and streetwise jazz.

At NEC, Schuller ushered John Lewis and the Modern Jazz Quartet into Jordan Hall. He encouraged composers and musicians mining the same vein, appointing Ran Blake, pianist and composer to lead its Third Stream program. Blake, whose musical interests echoed Schuller's, focused on the synthesis of different musics. He alchemized a new sound from the elements of Indian, African, folk, and ethnic music, insisting that to work in this expanded domain, musicians needed to find their own musical cores. As Peter Row put it, "You have to know it from the outside, and you have to hear it inside your head."

Third stream pedagogy was distinctively different, emphasizing intensive ear training. The program, still in a state of constant experiment and redefinition today, offered a haven for young artists who didn't fit into musical pigeonholes. Laurence Lesser later called it the school's "Research and Development" wing. One of its most successful ventures was the New England Conservatory Ragtime Ensemble. Formed and directed by Schuller, the ensemble enjoyed spectacular success, winning a Grammy for its 1974 recording of Scott Joplin rags. The ensemble appeared across America, most notably in Alice Tully Hall, on national television, and at the White House. Its whistle-stop tour of Russia made the group the most widely recognized interpreter of ragtime in the world.

Schuller's presidency, like Chadwick's, was convulsed by war. The Vietnamese conflict sparked bitter political anger unseen in earlier wars. The Conservatory was thrown into turmoil. Although not so radical as students in Madison, Berkeley, or Columbia, those at the Conservatory nonetheless clashed with tradition and authority.

In May 1969 the school's opera department presented Offenbach's satirical *Ba-Ta-Clan* at the Boston University Theater. Signs of political trouble appeared before the opera even opened. A guard, seeing a portrait of Mao Tse-tung, tried to stop what he feared was a revolution. Then the Students for a Democratic Society (SDS) weighed in, denouncing *Ba-Ta-Clan* as: "…a vicious attack upon the struggle of oppressed peoples throughout the world. For example, the Vietnamese people are made to look like clownish 'conspirators,' Black militants are made to look like stooges in pantaloons, revolutionary women are made to look like servants and can-can dancers, and the Chinese people's fight against U.S. imperialism is made to look like a vaudeville farce. This opera is an example of the way in which art can be used as propaganda attacking people's struggles with lies and distortions."

SDS members confronted Schuller, demanding that the Conservatory community discuss the production, then cancel it. Schuller obliged with an open discussion but refused to stop the performance, seeing in that demand an attack on artistic freedom.

Program cover for the NEC Ragtime Ensemble's 1974 performance of Scott Joplin tunes. That same year, the ensemble received a Grammy Award for its recording of Joplin songs.

Tensions rose at the Conservatory. Rumors swirled that the SDS, determined to cause trouble, intended to disrupt the opera. Administration officials arranged for police to be inconspicuously present and kept their own security guards on overtime. NEC students bought tickets to be in on the "fun." As political theater, the performance was a washout: neither the SDS nor the police left the wings. But the tension of the evening roused the cast to its finest performance. Worried critics disagreed about its political impact but testified to the production's "brilliant edginess."

The Conservatory meeting proved just as anticlimactic. Participants later described the drama as having three acts: a "surging release of pent-up feelings and emotions, a more reasoned and truly dialogic atmosphere," and a conclusion marked by "a certain lassitude if not boredom."

The *Ba-Ta-Clan* affair was merely a prelude. The United States' invasion of Cambodia in 1970 roused students and faculty across America to protest. Campuses were thrown into chaos. At Kent State University, National Guard troops shot four demonstrating students. Boston colleges went on strike. Vice-President Agnew attacked American's schools as "circus tents or psychiatric centers for overprivileged, underdisciplined, irresponsible children of the well-to-do blasé permissivists." And President Nixon, in his inimitable way, labeled the demonstrators as "bums blowing up the campuses."

The Conservatory dedicated its final concert that year to the students shot at Kent State. Students, faculty, and administrators met beforehand, agreeing to cancel auditions, recitals, and concerts to "protest U.S. actions in Asia, the repression of political prisoners like the Black Panthers, and war-related research at universities." Classes and exams were canceled. Students continued with their recitals, but they were neither graded nor sponsored by the Conservatory. While some students practiced, others formed a strike committee to organize the Conservatory's own unique protest: a marathon concert for peace. The concert began on May 10, 1970: a round-the-clock musical plea for peace and change.

The marathon briefly thrust Jordan Hall at NEC into the national spotlight. To protest the war, poets read verses, students played recitals or read aloud, teachers gave concerts, and jazz and rock groups from across the city performed. In the small hours of the morning, as a few sleepy students watched, the show went on. At other times, acclaimed performers roused a packed house: the cast of *Hair*, the "tribal rock musical" then being performed in Boston, sang a medley of its songs. It was political theater, and sleepless audiences roared their approval.

In those troubled days, the Conservatory drew together as a community. Although a few radicals pressed for militance, the majority were moderate but resolute. Proud of their marathon, students found in Jordan Hall at NEC a perfect rallying point for diverse audiences of musicians, teachers, and activists. In contravention of Boston's fire codes, Jordan Hall at NEC took on the atmosphere of a late-night jazz club: smoke from tobacco and less legal substances wreathed the air. The hall manager had a fit.

Next page: Schuller's New England Conservatory Ragtime Ensemble became enormously successful, appearing on national television and at the White House.

While political turmoil washed over the Conservatory, a more immediate problem was being worried out behind closed doors. The Board of Trustees brought the matter to a boil. For five tense years, the institution careened from one financial crisis to another.

The Conservatory produced a long run of annual deficits, making them up through fund-raising by friends and the Board of Trustees. In 1968 some trustees even proposed that the Conservatory should plan its budget on the assumption that the Vietnam War would be over in two years, thus freeing government money to flow back into education—and the Conservatory. There was no apparent method to this madness, nor any plan to put the institution on a sound fiscal footing. Schuller's artistic success had been bought at a steep price. Salaries and educational expenses rose 28 percent; tuition, only 5.6 percent. So the board yet again began to borrow. It took out mortgages of $313,000, then sold off $774,000 in invested funds. That dangerous game precipitated the Conservatory's terrible crisis in 1970–71. In-house accounting procedures were inadequate: annual financial reports predicted reduced deficits or even surpluses. The predictions were always wrong. So the deficit grew. In 1969 it climbed to $1.53 million; in 1970, to $1.82 million.

Not all the Conservatory news during that period was gloomy. The 1968 production of *Pelléas et Mélisande* at the Loeb Theater was a critical and popular success. The Conservatory's "artistic income" climbed, even as its fortunes fell. Interest in Schuller's new regime drew applications in record numbers: in 1967 the Conservatory had received only two hundred applications; a year later, ten times that. Schuller pressed his plans for making the Conservatory into a renowned international school of music, even as he admitted to trustees that its financial resources were at their nadir.

NEC was not alone. Juilliard and the Manhattan School of Music were just two of the many artistic institutions facing similar financial difficulties. Symphony orchestras, including Cleveland's, faced alarming deficits. But the Conservatory was in dire straits. Brokers from one private fund-raising company told Schuller that they knew of "no other institution with as serious a problem and they knew of no institution with as little Trustee support."

By then the Conservatory's survival was at stake. Some trustees urged a merger, but neither Boston University nor Massachusetts Institute of Technology would guarantee the school of music's survival, while Northeastern made no secret of coveting only its buildings. On February 24, 1970, their Executive Committee met with faculty and students in Jordan Hall at NEC. They revealed that the school was in danger and that there were no ready solutions. The shortsighted policies of the past had caught up with them. The endowment had languished since the 1930s. Now such a fund was desperately needed. But the trustees voiced their one strength. They were determined to keep the institution alive. They ruthlessly cut all program and operating budgets, mortgaged buildings for another $1 million, then took on the hard work of fund-raising, appealing to donors and national foundations.

They began their desperate strategy at the worst moment. By 1970 the economy was stalled in recession: grants, gifts, and funds dried up overnight. Then, as word spread of the Conservatory's financial problems, donors feared giving good money after bad. Trustees even fretted over the ethics of accepting gifts for a capital fund, when they were being swallowed up in operating expenses.

Worse news followed. The 1973 oil embargo battered the economy into a slump that lingered for the rest of the decade. It was in that climate that the trustees grasped their final straw: they would try to save the school with a massive fund drive, beginning with an appeal to the Ford Foundation.

So the trustees descended on Ford, then on the Mellon and Rockefeller foundations. The latter waited for Ford, and Ford insisted on seeing a sensible financial plan for the Conservatory. That sent the trustees back to the drawing board. Sherwin Badger, their chairman, gathered David Scudder, James Terry, Alan Morse, and Mrs. Frederick Stare to reorganize the trustees, bring in new blood, and devise more effective ways of making policy. They ordered the administration to produce a five-year plan acceptable to Ford, then searched out a wider circle of potential funders. Their cuts bit deeply. The community services mission was folded into the Extension Division, the Castle Hill program closed—the cafeteria even refused second helpings.

Despite their complaints about the food, students joined the effort. On their own initiative, they organized an Action Performance Committee to give concerts in local homes. By showing their talents and efforts, they hoped to convince Bostonians of the Conservatory's musicianship. They also hoped to raise money. More than 150 students, as well as faculty and staff, volunteered. Their efforts produced $3,200. Jan Gippo, a graduate student who chaired the program, recalled that he had never been involved in work "so informed by good will, unanimity of purpose, and the absence of infighting." Gerard Lennick, recruited to head a new endowment drive, saw a new determination at NEC: the school was suddenly and "totally mobilized toward saving itself."

Schuller led the way. He launched a national Start a Renaissance: Save the Conservatory campaign, taping television advertisements that appealed for help. Subway signs publicized the Conservatory's need and gathered support from within the community. But music best conveyed the message. The most powerful moment came at Christmas, when Conservatory students echoed Schuller's Renaissance campaign in seven concerts at the Prudential Center. Held a stone's throw from the site of the 1867 Jubilee, those concerts attracted more than 10,000 listeners and brought in $20,000 from 1,600 donors, given in amounts as large as $5,000 and as small as a dime. Back at Jordan Hall at NEC, the Conservatory initiated "discretionary donations" for its concerts. Schuller and Veronica Jochum von Moltke, the soloist, literally passed the hat after an orchestral concert, collecting $1,300.

Such efforts demonstrated the school's unity and determination, though the money did more to lift morale than reduce the deficit. Their work, however, was rewarded from an unexpected source. Mrs. John D. Rockefeller, a long-time friend of the Conservatory, bequeathed $1 million. That was a start, but it was not enough. The Ford Foundation followed, offering the prospect of a matching grant but insisted that school officials plan a $14-to-15-million endowment drive.

On March 29, 1971, the trustees drew up their new plan, then submitted it to the Foundation. Encouraged by signals from Ford, Schuller even announced a endowment campaign, which he opened by personally donating $5,000. The clouds began to part: a threatened strike by security guards evaporated, and Boston taxmen abandoned efforts to charge the Conservatory. Finally, Ford weigh in with a matching grant of $2.5 million, including $500,000 to pay off the mortgage; the remaining $2 million was targeted for endowment. As part of its grant, Ford required strict accounting, and the school's officers lived up to the terms. They brought the deficit down 13 percent in the first year, then another 15 percent in the second. Impressed by that show of financial discipline, the Mellon Foundation followed with a grant of $350,000 to discharge the remainder of the mortgage.

Sherwin Badger, chairman of the board, had saved the school. With the immediate danger past, he stepped down. William Driver, Jr., succeeded him, determined to continue Badger's work, but also to return music to the forefront. Schuller and Lorna Cooke deVaron took the Symphony Orchestra and Chorus on an epic tour of Europe in 1974. Although rumors of the "school in jeopardy" occasionally resurfaced, the music world saw that the Conservatory not only had saved itself but had become one of the most exciting schools in America.

NEC's financial troubles, however, were not yet over. No sooner had it invested its new endowment monies then the New York Stock Exchange plummeted, losing 30 percent of its value in one year. That catastrophe made the school's first annual report unhappy reading: even with the Ford money, the endowment had fallen by almost 11 percent. The subsequent oil embargo then plunged the economy deeper into recession. By June 1974 the Conservatory had again succumbed to deficit spending. By Christmas it was more than $1 million in the red. Once again the trustees were reduced to mortgaging the building to get through the year. But there was worse news. Midway through the matching drive for the Ford grant, only $500,000 of the $2 million had been raised.

One final crisis rocked the school. In December 1974, Gunther Schuller resigned, citing disagreements over the administrative reorganization drawn up by Donald Harris, the executive vice-president. Harris's plan had relieved Schuller of administrative worries by putting power in his own hands. The trustees hoped that would enable the president to devote more time and energy to the draining work of fund-raising, as well as to the more welcome tasks of composing, performing, and teaching. But the plan also cut a number of offices, including that of James Whitaker,

Schuller's longtime colleague and administrative coordinator. When the scheme had come before the Executive Committee, Schuller had approved it. But while recuperating from a minor operation, he changed his mind. Colleagues thought his decision reflected not his doubts about the plan but a more basic ambivalence about his new position. He no longer would be responsible for the day-to-day activities of the Conservatory, and that bothered him, even though he knew that other demands on his time made it impossible for him to exert effective control.

The *Boston Globe* reported his resignation and the acrimony it created in loving detail, providing more bad news for, and about, the Conservatory. So the board's chairman, William Driver, persuaded Schuller to withdraw his resignation. He did, but Harris's plan was jettisoned, Whitaker retained, and officials waited for the next shoe to fall.

On January 16, 1975, it did. Schuller called a Conservatory meeting, recapitulated the resignation flap, and announced that the essential subject of the meeting was yet another financial crisis: the school again faced catastrophic losses. As a step toward reducing them, Schuller announced cuts in administrative and teaching positions and wage freezes all across the Conservatory. He revealed that he had already frozen his own salary, then called upon the faculty to donate an extra hour each week, either by adding lessons or by taking on administrative tasks. He agreed that his measures were draconian but believed there was no choice. His news was somber. It left the community angry. Lost in the confusion of bad news was Schuller's revelation that he had also appointed a new director of administrative affairs, Andrew Falender, who came from the Department of Health, Education, and Welfare. His arrival was, to say the least, inauspicious, but it proved the best news NEC had heard in decades. Harris, who had hired him, promised a tumultuous time, and Schuller made sure of that.

Angry teachers began a drive to unionize under the auspices of the American Association of University Professors. For those who chafed under Schuller's tenure, the salary freeze had been the last straw. Alarmed by his dismissal of teachers, his autocratic rule, his idiosyncratic appointments, they believed that a union would protect them from caprice, provide health insurance and retirement funds benefits (neither of which NEC offered), and insulate them from tactics like the salary freeze.

For nine long months, debate over the issue of unionizing raged through the Conservatory's halls. Then on November 3, 1975, the faculty voted. Sixty-five of sixty-seven eligible voters appeared; forty-two of them voted the scheme down. The vote was a personal triumph for Schuller, but a larger, more important victory was in the offing.

Under Falender's ministrations, the budget improved dramatically. Trustees now gloried in the "superior management within the school" and the "uniquely early availability of the budget." They had given Falender final authority over all expenditure, and he wielded it to lop off spending. He reduced all budgetary expenses, increased enrollment, maintained the salary freeze,

and watched every item, from piano repairs to stationery supplies. His "tough budgets" and polite refusals to tolerate overspending became legendary, for he was determined to change the institution's tradition of bad financial habits.

His 1975 budget produced a $191,000 surplus, the first in almost two decades. From that point onward, NEC produced an unbroken string of surpluses. Falender also initiated the purchase of buildings on the other side of Huntington Avenue and on St. Botolph Street. His successful budgets and new buildings helped create a campus that anchored the Conservatory's educational mission and gave it a future.

In June 1977, Schuller brought his presidency to an end. After ten years in office he was determined to return to performing and composing. Before he left the stage, however, he had one last gesture to make—grand, exciting, and bold, typical of his presidency and of his previous standout concerts. He conducted Schoenberg's *Gurrelieder*, its first performance in Boston. Critics saw in the piece the emblems of Schuller's years at NEC. For Thor Eckert, Jr., in the Christian Science Monitor, it was a "a moving testament to this vibrant musician's contributions for [NEC] as well as for Boston." He thought it "incredible" that such an ambitious project could be accomplished by music students. For *Boston Globe* critic Richard Dyer, it was "leisurely, detailed, knowledgeable, and thrilling." And Ellen Pfeifer in the *Boston Herald* praised the orchestra "with its gorgeous strings and splendid brasses" and opined that "not many professional orchestras can ever hope to sound like that."

After the ambition and the flair of those years, distinguished critic Michael Steinberg gave the era a fitting epitaph: Schuller, he wrote, "though not free of controversy, has brought new musical life to the Conservatory and to Boston." In his own tribute, Chairman Driver said simply, "What he has set in motion here will endure and grow."

Andrew Falender, director of administrative affairs, was tough on overspending: in 1975 his budget produced a $191,000 surplus, the first in almost two decades.

Coda

The ideal music school in this country cannot arrive until conditions are made favorable to its growth and development. There are signs that these conditions are approaching…An ideal school…needs…expensive equipment. It needs artists and professors whose time and effort command large compensation, it needs permanent support from an enthusiastic art-loving public, and it needs an endowment fund large enough to provide for the entire education and maintenance of highly gifted young people.

—*George Chadwick (1908)*

After Schuller's departure, what the Conservatory needed was to consolidate his new ideas, as it had in the wake of Tourjée's and Chadwick's departures. So trustees selected a stabilizing force, J. Stanley Ballinger, as president. During his five-year term, the Conservatory held to its new direction. But personal difficulties weakened Ballinger's hold. In 1982 the trustees asked him to resign.

Under the steely financial regime of Board of Trustees Chairman Francis W. Hatch, Jr., and Administrative Affairs Director Andrew Falender, the Conservatory continued to produce an unbroken string of profits and prestige. Falender instilled the ethos of the balanced budget, while the trustees agreed to resume, yet again, their pursuit of an endowment. They had better luck, and greater response, than their predecessors. By 1985, the endowment was more than $21 million. In 1990 a second drive began to raise another $25 million of endowment, capital, and operating funds. Those campaigns shared the goals of previous failed efforts: to raise money for the equipment, scholarships, and salaries that would make NEC America's preeminent conservatory. But with better economic times, strong board leadership, and a better sense of the school's place in its community, the public gave its support.

While they searched for a successor to Ballinger, the trustees approved a novel administrative arrangement. They gave Falender, along with three faculty members —Laurence Lesser, Victor Rosenbaum, and Robert DiDomenica—shared responsibility. After a semester's trial of the so-called transition committee, they asked Lesser to be acting president (his actual title was artistic director). When the search for a president was extended even longer, they eventually asked Lesser to become the new president.

As an internationally renowned cellist and former student of Gregor Piatigorsky, as well as a Phi Beta Kappa Harvard mathematics major, Lesser combined executive and artistic talents and joined the long line of Conservatory leaders who had emerged from faculty ranks. Inaugurated in 1983, he shared authority with Falender, who as chief executive officer was responsible for the business side of the Conservatory. That arrangement lasted until 1988, when Falender left and Lesser assumed the full administrative burden.

So New England Conservatory took on a new leader, a new role, and a renewed sense of purpose. The Conservatory's last thirteen years can be characterized as a steady but inexorable flow toward excellence and stability. All aspects of the Conservatory have improved, from the quality of its students and faculty, the maintenance of the facility, the restoration of Jordan Hall at NEC, and the acquisition of adjoining properties, to the diversity of cultures and nations represented, the visible and audible concertizing locally, nationally, and internationally, the successful return of opera, and a completed capital campaign, the largest in the institution's history.

After NEC emerged from the fog of fiscal insecurity of the 1970s and began to stabilize under the Falender regime of budget surpluses, the trustees and administration, led by Hatch, Falender, and Lesser, began to build the Conservatory's position. One opportunity dropped into their laps when the building across the street, 295 Huntington Avenue, was for sale. They bought it in 1982 and after some refurbishment moved several administrative offices and classrooms to portions of the new building.

An even greater opportunity arose when the nearby Cotting School for Handicapped Children, on St. Botolph Street, came on the market. Anxious moments and negotiations came to fruition when the Conservatory managed to buy the property ahead of the deeper pockets of other institutions. It was a large stretch, one that required even tighter budgets, but it made possible for the first time the true beginnings of a realistic campus for the Conservatory, one that would eventually fill all its needs. The building provided classrooms, rehearsal and performance space, administrative offices, and rental space (primarily to Northeastern University for a few years). With the addition of the "St. Botolph building," as it became known,

NEC had a unified campus. It is the field of dreams for President Lesser, who sees the adjacent parking lot as a site for another building that would complete the Conservatory's community: dormitory rooms suitable for individual practice, a reunited library, a theater suitable for opera, faculty offices, and all-purpose common rooms. (The unattractive 1960s dormitory would disappear to make all that possible.)

Real estate ventures were the outward signs of a burgeoning confidence within the Conservatory based on a solid fiscal foundation and on the gradual, quietly dramatic improvement in the quality of students attracted to NEC. During the doleful years of the 1980s demographic drought in eligible high school graduates, NEC found itself anxiously wondering whether talented students were out there and whether they would come. They did, in increasing numbers. Applications increased every year, and so did quality. At the end of the 1980s, a decade that prognosticators had pronounced as dire, NEC glowed in solid enrollments and a student population deeper in quality than ever before and more diverse as well.

One of the streams that fed the tide of rising excellence was a return from an investment Eben Tourjée made in the 1870s, when he sent Luther Mason to Japan to teach music. ("Mason-song" became part of the local argot in Japan for school children learning music.) Students from Asia—Japan, South Korea, Taiwan, China, Hong Kong, Singapore—suddenly made NEC their school of choice. Attracted by teachers of international reputation, those students soon reached more than a quarter of the total enrollment. Although they had to cope with studies in a new language, they brought a vital international perspective that created a rapid change in the culture of the Conservatory. Students also began to arrive in increasing numbers from Europe, South America, and even distant Australia.

While the quality of the students continued to improve, the quality of programs improved also. Significantly, graduate programs attracted students of broader and deeper quality, the return of the opera program in 1989 being a standout, recently joined by an innovative program in jazz in collaboration with the Thelonious Monk Institute of Jazz Performance. In addition, the Artist Diploma became significantly more selective and is now a very exclusive club, attracting the elite of young artists. As a capstone to the graduate programs and the fulfillment of many long-held dreams, the doctoral program was inaugurated.

At the same time graduate studies at the Conservatory expanded during the late 1980s and early 1990s, the undergraduate program also underwent extensive revision, especially in the academic arena. Recognizing that the vision of the complete musician that still reverberated from the Schuller years could not be accomplished with only excellence in musical pedagogy, faculty strengthened and integrated academic courses to better prepare undergraduates for their musical studies and for the larger world within which they would follow their profession. Their efforts were rewarded with major grants from the National Endowment for the Humanities, the first such national recognition of the Conservatory's attempts to strive for academic excellence.

NEC has emphasized college activity as the traditional focus, but the Extension Division, under the leadership of its dean, Mark Churchill, has also grown to be a vital part of the Conservatory. It extends its reach in two ways: to the preparatory school, including a cooperative program at the Walnut Hill School, and to the community of Boston.

At Walnut Hill, young musicians from around the world are "prepared" to study at NEC and other leading schools of music and colleges throughout the country. Such an idea—early preparation for advanced musical study—has been an important part of NEC's history from the very beginning. Tourjée had feeder schools in Providence, he ran summer schools for younger students, and, of course, most important, Lowell Mason and his brother devised and ran the first music programs for Boston public schools in the nation.

Laurence Lesser

The Extension Division faces in the same direction as those pioneering Mason brothers: to the local schools of Boston and to the communities around them. Adult education programs make Conservatory-taught courses accessible. And two major initiatives developed over the past five years involve the Conservatory and other major cultural institutions, including the BSO and WGBH, in music programs in Boston schools.

While NEC has reached out in those essential ways, it has also been busy concertizing. Every two years, the NEC Youth Philharmonic Orchestra from the Preparatory School, under conductor Benjamin Zander, performs on tour. Recently acclaimed concerts include Israel, Argentina, Chile, and Europe. In 1994 the NEC Orchestra first made its way to Carnegie Hall in a tribute to Piatigorsky made possible through the cellist's family. The NEC Big Band performs regularly at jazz festivals. The Klezmer Conservatory Band was an integral part of *Schlemiel* at the American Repertory Theatre in Cambridge, a show slated for Broadway. One of the most highly acclaimed young string quartets, the Borromeo Quartet, forged in the crucible of NEC's Artist Diploma program, is gaining a worldwide reputation while in residence at NEC. A program to bring famous composers to NEC for residencies has brought such luminaries as John Cage, Sir Michael Tippett, György Ligeti, Olivier Messiaen, Leon Kirchner, and Witold Lutoslawski. And in addition to the 450-odd free concerts provided by NEC every year, a focused festival week in the spring continues to explore a major theme, such as Latin American music and the role of the Jewish composer, or the works of a single musician, such as John Cage.

The Conservatory's influence reaches beyond the United States. In 1991 a group of NEC students traveled to Moscow as part of the Making Music Together series originated by NEC alumna Sarah Caldwell. Being in Moscow during the troubled collapse of the former Soviet Union provided a unique experience beyond the music making. Return visits on Jordan Hall's stage by Russian artists led to the first appearance in the West of violist Yuri Bashmet and composer Giya Kancheli. Japanese students and faculty from Toho Music School in Toyko visited NEC in 1991, and NEC students reciprocated in Tokyo in 1993.

President Lesser emphasized the vital importance of the faculty and attracted excellent performers and teachers to NEC: James Buswell, Colin Carr, Donald Palma, Stephen Drury, Lee Hyla, Kathleen Kaun, Richard Hughes, Marcus Thompson, Irma Vallecillo, Michèle Auclair, and the return of Scott Nickrenz and Paula Robison. The Conservatory lost three of its most famous teachers: Sherman Walt and Harold Wright, both prominent members of the BSO, and Louis Krasner, one of the great teachers of his generation. Fortunately, Eugene Lehner, another Conservatory treasure, is still active. Lorna Cooke deVaron retired with Emerita status after more than forty years on the faculty. Tamara Brooks took over the NEC Chorus.

The return of John Moriarty marked another try at opera. Many times in the past, predecessors had tried to establish an opera program and many times the venture had proven unworkable, either from lack of voices, lack of performance space, or expenses. This time, Moriarty succeeded brilliantly. The strong upsurge of enrollment and talent in voice at NEC is at least in part because of

the highly competitive opera program. Persistence over a hundred years is paying off. Likewise for Chadwick's great project, the orchestra. In 1992 Richard Hoenich of the Montreal Symphony assumed leadership of the orchestral program after a period under the direction of young BSO conductors Pascal Verrot and Carl St. Clair. The orchestra's excellence is now taken for granted.

These many steps toward consolidation and stability, as well as NEC's historic influence and import, received national recognition in the spring of 1994, when the United States Park Service conferred National Historic Landmark status on New England Conservatory, the only music school in America to be so honored. And, in a rare dual designation, its incomparable concert hall became a Landmark as well. In the nomination papers the Park Service historian noted: "the history of New England Conservatory and the history of Jordan Hall ... have been inseparable."

Presently, Jordan Hall at NEC clatters with jackhammers and shrieks with buzz saws. Broken bricks are piled in the corridors, dust billows out the windows, and the empty hall echoes to the cacophony of construction. Soon, however, the opening of the refurbished hall will take on some of the strains of the original opening back on that cool evening on October 20, 1903. Cars, not the hansoms of old, will jam Huntington Avenue and Gainsborough Street. Music lovers and eminent citizens will come to support NEC and see the bright shining hall restored to its original colors. They will hear the NEC Orchestra play on the newly finished stage, and they will hear prestigious performers such as Yo-Yo Ma and Wynton Marsalis.

Yet the next morning, the practice rooms will be full at six o'clock. Lessons and classes will fill the day. The orchestra will assemble to begin new rehearsals. The pulse of music will go on. Renewing and restoring Jordan Hall at NEC is a major step in the process of educating musicians, apprentices to their craft being transformed into artists through the ancient and human glories of teaching and learning and making music.

Appendix

Bibliography

Aliferis Memorandum. 16 September 1991.

Amory, Cleveland. *The Proper Bostonian.*
New York: E.P. Dutton and Co., 1947.

Bartlett, James C. "Reminiscences of Early
Conservatory Experiences." *New England Conservatory
Alumni Opus,* 1951.

The Boston Globe, 21 October 1903; 22 May 1942;
8 and 9 May 1970; 17 January 1971.

Brookline Chronicle, 27 August 1931.

Chadwick, George Whitefield. Letter to Theodore
Thomas. Chadwick Papers. 15 December 1894,
21 February 1894, 21 February 1897, 25 March 1899,
21 November 1902.

"Conservatories." *The Musical Courier,* 14 March 1900.

Denée, Charles. "Denée on Tourjée." In "For God and
Music: The Life Story of Eben Tourjée, Father of the
American Conservatory." Written by Leo Eben Tourjée.
Address delivered at commemoration of 100th
anniversary of Eben Tourjée's birth, Jordan Hall at
New England Conservatory, Boston, 1 June 1934.

Dwight's Journal of Music, 1852-1879.

Fitzpatrick, John Edward. "The Music Conservatory
in America." Ph.D. diss., Boston University, 1963.

Garofalo, Robert Joseph. *Frederick Shepherd Converse
(1871-1940): His Life and Music.* Metuchen, N.J.:
Scarecrow Press, 1994.

Glackens, Ira. *Yankee Diva: Lillian Nordica and the
Golden Days of Opera.* New York: Coleridge Press, 1963.

Grove, Sir George. *Grove's Dictionary of Music and
Musicians.* Edited by Eric Blom. New York: St. Martins
Press, 1954.

Horowitz, Joseph. *New York Times,* 27 October 1991.

Kimball, T.C. Testimony. *Boston Transcript,*
6 February 1889.

Lesser, Laurence. Interview. July 1991.

Musical Herald, January 1882, June 1884, August 1884,
July 1885, March 1886, August 1886, September 1886,
December 1886, August 1887, October 1887.

Netsky, Hankus. "Program Notes," *Jazz and Third
Stream Festival,* New England Conservatory,
27 February-2 March 1989.

Neume, 1907, 1910.

New England Conservatory Administrative Policy
Committee Minutes, 23 December 1946.

New England Conservatory Board of Trustees Minutes,
21 February, 7 October, 17 November 1941; 1 May,
16 June 1942; 19 March, 14 May, 22 June 1943;
17 March, 27 October, 1 December 1944; 12 June,
26 October, 14 December 1945; 22 April, 26 October,
13 December 1946; 7 February, 17 June, 24 October,
12 December 1947; 9 April, 8 October 1948; 21 June 1949;
1 December 1950; 2 November 1951; 1 April, November 5
1955; 13 April 1956; 1 November 1957;
23 July 1963; 7 November 1968.

New England Conservatory Bulletin, May 1897;
May 1908; September, October 1914; September, October,
December 1917; September 1920; March, August 1922;
March, December 1925; March 1926; November 1927;

April, July, September, October 1928; November 1933; August 1934; May, November, December 1935; February 1936; January, November 1938; May, November 1939; February 1940; April, July/August, December 1942; April, June, August, December 1943; June, August, September, October 1944; February 1945; March, October 1946; October 1947; March 1949; December 1950; Fall 1955; Winter/Spring, 1956; Fall 1958; Spring 1959; Fall 1960; September 1963; 1968-1969.

New England Conservatory Calendar. 1887-1888.

New England Conservatory Director's Report, 1921-22, 1931-32, 1932-33, 1933-34, 1934-35, 1935-36, 1936-37, 1937-38, 1938-39, 1939-40, 1940-41.

New England Conservatory Endowment Committee Minutes, 15 February 1937.

New England Conservatory Executive Committee Minutes, 1939-1976.

New England Conservatory Finance Committee Minutes, 7 February 1935; 18 January, 4 June 1937; 3 March, 14 April 1939; 13 June 1942; 27 October 1944; 18 April 1949; 17 February 1961; 29 September 1967.

New England Conservatory Magazine, February 1898, May 1898, May 1900, March 1901, July 1902, October 1902, December 1902, March 1903, November 1903, April 1911.

New England Conservatory Policy Committee Minutes, October 1942, January 1945

New England Conservatory Review, October 1898, May 1912.

New England Survey Committee Minutes, 25 January 1937.

Schuller, Gunther. Centennial address at Jordan Hall at New England Conservatory, Boston, 16 February 1967.

Schuller, Gunther. Letter to Board of Trustees, 27 May 1969.
Schuller, Gunther. Address to Combined Faculty and

Staff Meeting, 16 December 1974, 16 February 1975.

Still, William Grant. Interview by R. Donald Brown, 13 November 1967 and 4 December 1967. Fulerton Oral History Program, California State University.

Talley, Gordon. "Source of Splendid Sound." *Tribute to Jordan Hall,* 10 February 1991.

Tourjée, Leo Eben. "For God and Music: The Life Story of Eben Tourjée, Father of the American Conservatory." Thesis. Photocopy.

Williams, Chester W. *Indeed Music: My Years at New England Conservatory.* Boston: New England Conservatory, 1989.

Yellin, Victor Fell. *Chadwick: Yankee Composer.* Washington, D.C.: Smithsonian Institution Press, 1990.

Index

Abe, Seige, 88

Academy of Music, 20

A.D. 1919 (Parker), 88

Adamowski
    Antoinette Szumowska
        See Szumowska-Adamowski,
        Antoinette Timothée, 42, 44, 47, 49,
        56, 70

Adams, Elwyn, 119

African American students, 118, 119, 134

A.H.M. (music critic, Boston Transcript), 88

Aïda, 102

Albert Herring (Britten), 115

Aldrich, William T., 120

Alexander Balus (Handel), 114

Alexander II, 76

Alice Tully Hall, 136

Aliferis, James, 123-127

Aliferis Music Achievement Test, 123

Alleluia (Bach), 126

Allen, Philip
    appoints Keller, Harrison, 120
    background and character, 95
    endowment, 95, 108
    finances, 113
    length of service, 119
    praise for, 93
    retires, 120
    mentioned, 129

Alpha Chi Omega, 75

Alumni Association, 53

American Academy of Arts and Letters, 57

American Association of University Professors, 143

American Conservatory at Fontainebleau, 103

American music
    Chadwick, George Whitefield champions, 79
    during World War I, 83
    jazz, 133
    NEC Orchestra and, 87-89
    Newman, Ruby and, 99
    pre-Civil War tastes in, 20

American Opera Company, 43

American Repertory Theatre, 147

American Rubber Company, 73

Ames, Governor, 45

Anderson, Marian, 118, 121

annual festivals, 126, 133, 147

Anthony, Susan B., 76

Apollo Club, 55

Ariadne auf Naxos (Strauss), 108, 115

Armstrong, Louis, 86

Astor, Mary, 88

Athenaeum, 68

Atkins, Carl, 133

Auclair, Michele, 147

Austen, Ruth Elizabeth, 89

Bach, Johann Sebastian, 126

Badger, Sherwin, 125-127, 141

Baermann, Carl, 53

Bailey, Lillian, 43

Ballantine, Edward, 89

Ballinger, J. Stanley, 144

Barber, Samuel, 113

Barnum, P.T., 20

Baroque music, 103

Bartered Bride (Smetana), 115

Bartók, Béla, 87, 114

Bashmet, Yuri, 147

Ba-Ta-Clan affair, 136, 137

Battisti, Frank, 135

Beach, Amy, 51, 52, 77

Beautiful Munich (Chadwick), 55

Beck, Conrad, 114, 127

Beethoven, Ludwig van, 60, 88, 114

Beethoven statue, 18, 68

Bell, Alexander Graham, 30

Beneficent Society, 75

Berg, Alban Maria Johannes, 86

Berklee College of Music, 133

Berkshire Music Center, 99, 114

Berlioz, Hector, 114

Bernstein, Leonard, 104, 123, 128

Big Band, NEC, 147

Bimboni, Oreste, 60, 61, 70, 102

Bizet, Georges, 111

Black Panthers, 137

Blake, Ran, 135, 136

Bloomer, Amelia, 76

Boatwright, McHenry, 115, 119

Bok, Mary Curtis, 94

Bolero (Ravel), 133

Borromeo Quartet, 147

Boston, racial strife in, 135

Boston Conservatory of Music, 18, 24, 51

Boston Evening Transcript, 88, 89

Boston Federal Reserve, 95

Boston Globe
    Bernstein, Leonard reviewed, 104
    Jordan Hall, 13, 68
    NEC students during World War II, 106
    Quartet for the End of Time reviewed, 117
    Schuller, Gunther, 142, 143
    Sleeper Hall reviewed, 42

Boston Herald, 113, 143

Boston Opera Company, 24, 85, 93, 99

Boston Opera House
    closed and razed, 115
    photo of, 71, 80, 100, 101
    mentioned, 81, 89

Boston Orchestra Club, 47

Boston String Quartet, 95, 120, 125, 127

Boston Students' Union, 94

Boston Symphony Orchestra (BSO)
    alliance with NEC, 24, 28, 29, 51, 104
    Burgin, Richard and, 120
    Chadwick, George Whitefield and, 55, 56
    Cooke deVaron, Lorna and, 114, 128
    during World War I, 83-85, 87
    endowed, 21
    Gericke, Wilhelm and, 39, 43, 56
    Higginson, Henry L. and, 14, 28
    joint performance with NEC chorus, 78
    Jordan Hall inaugural, 13, 69
    Koussevitzky, Serge joins, 87
    Muck, Karl and, 78
    photo of, 28
    Schaefer, Lois and, 121
    mentioned, 64, 65, 70, 89, 113, 146, 147

Boston Theatre, 60, 61

Boston Transcript, 78, 88

Boston University, 21, 29, 40, 50, 110, 140

Boulanger, Nadia, 103, 121

Brahms, Johannes, 79

Braxton, Anthony, 134

British War Relief, 105

Brookmeyer, Bob, 134

Brooks

    Esther, 125

    Phillips, 42

    Tamara, 147

Brown

    Edwin, 93, 95, 119

    George W., 90, 91, 93, 119

Brown Hall, 73, 90, 91, 94, 106, 125

Bruckner, Anton, 113, 127

Brüll, Ignaz, 61

Bryan, William Jennings, 75

Bryn Mawr, 114

Büchtiger, Fritz, 114, 128

Bulletin, 95, 97

Bülow, Hans von, 22, 79

Burgin, Richard, 120, 121, 125, 127

Busoni, Ferruccio, 15, 50, 51, 77

Buswell, Jamie, 147

Byard, Jaki, 134

Byun, Wya-Kyung, 135

Cage, John, 147

Caldwell, Sarah, 110, 115, 147

Cammaerts, Emile, 86

Campanari, Leandro, 38, 42, 44

Carmen (Bizet), 111, 115

Carnegie Hall, 146, 147

Carr

    Colin, 147

    Samuel, 90, 91, 94

Carter, Elliott, 121

Casals, Pablo, 15

Castle Hill Summer Program, 128, 141

Castle Square Opera Company, 51

Catacoustical Measures (Pinkham), 127

CBS Radio Network, 97

Ceely, Robert, 128

centennial, 128, 132

Chadwick, George Whitefield

    accomplishments, 70, 73

    African American students, 118

    ambitions for NEC, 90, 91

    background and character, 55-58, 64, 75, 77

    Chicago World Fair, 55, 56

    competition from other schools, 94

    degree granting authority, 89

    dies, 91

    during World War I, 84

    Faelten, Carl, relations with, 53

    historical context of, 58

Chadwick, George Whitefield *(Continued)*

    ideal music school, 144

    Jordan, Eben, 2nd, and, 64

    Jordan Hall, plans and building of, 64, 65, 67

    Jordan Hall, use of, 78

    Jordan Hall inaugural, 13, 14, 69

    Jordan Hall organ, 68

    length of service, 119

    musical tastes and programming of, 58, 79, 86, 87, 89

    opera, 60, 61

    orchestra, 59, 77, 88

    photo of, 54, 56, 59

    retires, 91, 93

    sets rigorous standards, 89

    works-*Beautiful Munich*, 55

        Elegy, 88

        Euterpe, 79

        First Symphony, 55

        Harmony, 56

        Marguerita, 55

        Melpomene, 14, 46, 55, 56, 69

        Ode, 56

        Padrone, The, 79

        Quartet No. 3, 56

        Quartet No. 5, 56

        Rip Van Winkle, 91

        Suite Symphonic, 79

        Tam O'Shanter, 79

        Third Symphony, 56

        Viking's Last Voyage, 55

    mentioned, 15, 46, 87, 88, 95, 102, 104, 106, 111, 113, 116, 125, 129, 132-134, 147

Chadwick Medal, 119

Chamber Music Society (Boston), 49

Chamber Music Society of Lincoln Center, 111

Chants de Mer, Les (Gaubert), 104

Chevalier of the Legion of Honor, 87

Chicago Festival, 60

Chicago Opera, 24

Chicago Opera Company, 84

Chicago World's Fair, 55, 76

China, 105, 116

Chodos, Gabriel, 135

choral societies, Tourjée, Eben promotes formation of, 31

Chow, Idella, 105

Christian Science Monitor, 143

Christian Yenching College (Beijing), 105

Churchill, Mark, 146

Cincinnati Conservatory, 20

Cincinnati Symphony, 131

Civil War, 17, 18, 21, 33

Classical Symphony (Prokofiev), 108

class system, 17, 21

Claus, J.B., 44, 45, 47

Cleveland Institute of Music, 99

Cleveland Orchestra, 104

Cloak, The (Puccini), 115, 128

Cogan, Robert, 128, 133

Cohan, Robert, 125

community service, 134, 135, 141

Concertino (Converse), 104

Concerto for Orchestra (Kohs), 108

Concerto for Violin (Glazunov), 108

Concerto in F (Rheinberger), 60

Conducting an Amateur Orchestra (Holmes), 113

conservatories and schools of music, 20, 94, 140. See also specific conservatories

Conservatory Band, 98

Converse, Frederick

    as composer of American music, 88

    as student of Chadwick, George Whitefield, 56, 57

    criticism of his composing, 79

    NEC hires, 70

    photo of, 57

    works

        Concertino, 104

        Jeanne d'Arc, 78

        Job, 78

        Mystic Trumpeter, 97

        Pipe of Desire, 78

        Sacrifice, 78

        Symphony in D, 70

    mentioned, 15, 87, 102

Cook, Thomas, 29

Cooke deVaron, Lorna

    Aliferis, James and, 125

    becomes choral director, 114

    honorary degree, 121

    photo of, 114, 115

    retired, 147

    Soviet tour, 128

    tours Europe with NEC Chorus, 142

    work with Holmes, Malcolm, 114

    mentioned, 127, 133

Copland, Aaron

    at Jordan Hall, 117

    Boulanger, Nadia and, 103

Copland, Aaron (Continued)
    honorary degree, 121
    Second Hurricane, 104
    mentioned, 89, 113, 114, 122
Corelli
    Arcangelo, 104
    Franco, 125
Costume Carnival, 75
Cotting School for Handicapped Children, 145
Covent Garden, 99
Cowell, Stanley, 134
Cowles Art School, 69
Cox, Jena, 115
Crawford, Thomas, 68, 69
Crucible (Ward), 115
culture, post-Civil War, 19
curriculum. See also specific subject area
    changes under Aliferis, James, 123-125
    contemporary music, 103
    musical theory strengthened, 70, 124
    under Chadwick, George Whitefield, 70, 89
    under Faelten, Carl, 51
    under Goodrich, John Wallace, 97
    under Schuller, Gunther, 132
    under Williams, Chester, 126
Curtin, Phyllis, 110
Curtis Institute of Music, 94

Dalcroze, Jaques, 70, 124
Dallapiccola, Luigi, 114, 132, 133
d'Amboise, Jacques, 125
Dana, Richard Henry, Jr.
    Chadwick, George Whitefield and, 55
    Faelten, Carl and, 53
    funding, 46
    resigns as president, 63
    mentioned, 13, 40, 65
Dana Hall, 94
Daniel Jazz (Gruenberg), 120
Daniels, Mabel Wheeler, 56, 57, 77, 113
Daphnis and Chloé (Ravel), 114
Davis, Maude Reese, 77
Death over Basel (Beck), 114, 127
Debussy, Claude, 86, 87
Deep Forest (Daniels), 113
De la Mare, Walter, 70
Denée, Charles, 22, 53
Denée Cup, 75
de Pasquale, Joseph, 127
Depression era, 93-98

Deserts (Varése), 127
DeVita, Emmalina, 108
Diamond, David, 103, 108, 113
Dickson, Harry Ellis, 15
DiDomenica, Robert, 135, 144
Ditson, Oliver, 17, 18, 20, 35
Dives and Lazarus (Vaughan Williams), 108
Dixon, James, 125, 126
Dohnányi, Ernö 117, 122
Domingo, Placido, 110
Don Giovanni, 115
dormitories
    construction in the 1950s, 124
    during the 1940s and 1950s, 122, 123
    photo of new, under construction, 112
Driver, William, Jr., 142, 143
Drury, Stephen, 147
Dunham, Henry
    African American students, 118
    after the death of Tourjée, Eben, 49
    Faelten, Carl, relations with, 53
    inaugural recital, 67
    Music Hall organ, 68
    orchestra work, 44
    World War I, 83
    mentioned, 45, 70
Duryea, Reverend, 33, 36, 38
Dvorák, Antonín, 56, 73, 75
Dwight, John
    Chadwick, George Whitefield and, 56
    Jordan Hall inaugural, 13
    musical tastes, 20, 26, 28, 29
    photo of, 18
    Tourjée, Eben and, 17, 18
Dwight's Journal of Music
    comments on NEC, 37
    criticism of early NEC concerts, 24
    criticism of pre-Civil War music, 20
    Dwight, John as editor of, 17
    music in America, 58
    Peace Jubilees, 27
    photo of, 18
    reports opening and inaugural concert of NEC, 18, 19

early music, 132
ear training, 136
Easter Cantata (Pinkham), 114
East Greenwich Academy, 20, 30, 37
Eastman, George, 94
Eastman School of Music, 94, 121
Eckert, Thor, Jr., 143

Egmont (Beethoven), 60
Eichberg, Julius, 18, 24, 27, 44, 51
electronic music, 127
Elégie Française (Lévy), 108
Elegy (Chadwick), 88
Elgař, Edward, Sir, 86
Elias, Rosalind, 110, 111
Ellington, Duke, 118
Elma Lewis School of Fine Arts, 134
Elson, Louis, 42, 44
Emerson College of Oratory, 69
Emerson Majestic Theatre, 81
Emmanuel, Victor, 38
endowment
    1917 drive, 73, 75
    1937 drive, 95
    Allen, Philip works for, 108, 120
    critical need for, recognized, 129
    Ford Foundation insists on, drive, 141, 142
    languished since the 1930s, 140
    work continues, 144
enrollment
    1957, 123
    1960s, 129
    1980s, 145
    during first year, 19, 22
    early, of wind and string players, 44
    falls, 52, 94, 123
    fluctuations in, 37
    grows, 90, 143
    international students, 116
    Korean War and, 122
    under Aliferis, James, 126
    World War II
        after, 107, 113, 117
        during, 99, 105
Estabrook, Arthur, 13
Esterhazy Orchestra, 128
Étude, Presser, Theodore founds, 29
Eugene Onegin (Tchaikovsky), 102, 115
eurhythmics, 70, 124, 128
Euterpe (Chadwick), 79
Evans
    Gil, 134
    Mrs. Robert, 73, 75
Extension Division, 135, 141, 146

Faelten, Carl
    as director of NEC, 49-53
    background and character, 49, 50, 53
    compared to Chadwick, George Whitefield, 57

Faelten, Carl (*Continued*)
    Hale, Frank, relations with, 51, 53
    historical context of, 58
    joins NEC, 38
    link with BSO, 104
    music philosophy of, 49
    opera, 50, 60
    photo of, 50
    Sleeper Hall inaugural, 42
    star system, criticizes, 40
    mentioned, 47, 56, 63
Fairbanks, Douglas, Jr., 106
Falender, Andrew, 142-145
Fall River Musical Institute, 20
Fantasie Humoresque (Shepherd), 79
Fantasie in the Form of a Sonata (Saran), 24
Farrar, Geraldine, 83
Fauré, Gabriel, 102, 103
Faust, 99, 115
Faust, Oliver, 69
Faust School of Piano Tuning, 69
Feathertop (Hawthorne), 88
Federal Bureau of the Arts, 96
Federal Emergency Relief Administration
    (FERA), 96
Federal Youth Administration, 97
Feminine Mystique (Friedan), 117
Fenno, Pauline, 96
Fenway, as cultural center, 89
Festival of New England Music, 113
Fifth Symphony (Beethoven), 88
Figaro (Mozart), 107, 114, 115
Firestone
    Harvey S., Jr., 125
    Idabelle, 125
Firestone Tire & Rubber Company, 125
First Symphony (Chadwick), 55
First Symphony (Mahler), 133
First Symphony (Schuller), 135
First Symphony (Shostakovich), 108
Fisk Jubilee Singers, 118
Fletcher Musical System, 70
Floyd, Carlisle, 115, 126
football, influence on music, 98
Foote, Arthur, 15, 56, 79, 113
Ford Foundation, 123, 134, 140, 141
Fortunato, D'Anna, 111
Founder's Day, 75
Fourth Symphony (Session), 127
Foy, Cora Calvert, 77
Franck, César, 78, 102, 104
fraternities, 75. See specific organization
Fremont-Smith, Maurice, 125, 133

French National Radio Orchestra, 132
Fries, Wulf, 49
Frost, Rufus, 40, 45, 46, 63, 65
Frost Hall, 94
Frostiana (Thompson), 114
Fulbright scholars, 116, 119

Gardner
    Charles, 13, 40, 63, 65, 67
    Isabella Stewart, 13, 65, 87
Gardner Hall, 94
Gateway of Isphael (Foote), 79
"*Genealogy of Nineteenth Century Violinists,*
    A" (Austen), 89
Gericke, Wilhelm
    at NEC, 43
    conducts *Melpomene*, 56
    debuts *Symphony in D*, 70
    Jordan Hall inaugural, 14, 69
    link between BSO and NEC, 104
    photo of, 14, 43
    staffs BSO with European musicians, 39,
       43
    mentioned, 113
German music, 103
Gershwin, George, 89, 120
G.I. Bill, 107, 113
Gilbert, Clayton, 61
Gillespie, Dizzy, 134
Gilmore, Patrick, 26, 27, 29, 77, 99
Giuffre, Jimmy, 134
Gladys Childs Miller Scholarship Fund, 111
Glazunov, Alexander, 108
Glimmerglass Opera, 111
Gluck, Christoph Willibald, 78
Goldbeck, Robert, 18, 19, 21
Golden Cross (Brüll), 61
Golden Prince (Hadley), 79
Goldovsky, Boris
    after World War II, 107
    at Castle Hill Summer Program, 128
    background and character, 99
    Dohnányi, Ernö duet, 122
    honorary degree, 121
    influence on NEC vocal program, 109-111
    "Opera on the Air," 102, 109
    photo of, 109, 119
    productions staged by, 115
    size of productions, 114, 115
    starts NEC Opera School, 99, 102
    starts New England Opera Theater, 110
    mentioned, 117, 120, 128
Goldovsky Opera Institute, 102

Goldovsky Opera Theater, 115
Goodman, Benny, 99
Goodrich, John Wallace
    accomplishments of, 104
    African American students, 118
    as student of Chadwick, George
      Whitefield, 56, 57
    background and character, 93, 96
    Chadwick Memorial Concert, 91
    contemporary music, 103
    during the Depression, 96, 97
    during World War I, 86
    French government honors, 87
    innovation through technology, 97
    Jordan Hall inaugural, 13
    length of service, 119
    musical tastes of, 89, 98, 104
    NEC Orchestra and, 88
    opera, 61, 78, 99, 102
    performances at Jordan Hall, 78
    photo of, 89, 116
    plays for Governor Ames, 45
    resigns as director, 102, 104
    support for contemporary music, 102
    World War II, 106
    mentioned, 70, 116, 120, 126
graduation rates, 37, 44, 46, 117
Graham, Martha, 125
Grainger, Percy, 79
Grammy Award, 136
Grant, Ulysses S., 27
Greek letter societies, 75. See also specific
    organization
Grieg, Edvard, 42
Gurrelieder (Schoenberg), 143

Hadley, Henry, 79, 88
Haffner Symphony (Mozart), 133
Hale
    Edward, 51
    Frank, 49, 51-53
    Philip, 56, 78
Hamilton, Hadley, 77
Hammerstein, Oscar, 60
Handel, George Frideric, 42
    works
      Alexander Balus, 114
Handel & Haydn Society, 22, 51, 55, 58, 68
Hänsel und Gretel, 99-101, 128
Harmonic Idiom of the Jazz Orchestra, The
    (Tesson), 128
Harmony (Chadwick), 56
Harriet Spaulding Charitable Trust, 123

Harris, Donald, 132, 142

Hartmann, Karl, 127

Harvard Lampoon Building, 81

Harvard Musical Association, 13, 17, 22, 47, 55, 58

Harvard University, 14, 47, 69, 89

Hastreiter, Helene, 43

Hatch, Francis W., Jr., 144, 145

Haven and Hoyt, 91

Hawthorne, Nathaniel, 68, 88

Haydn, Franz Joseph, 60

Hayes, Roland, 118

Heiss, John, 135

Henley, W.E., 70

Henschel

    George, 43, 70

    Lillian Bailey, 43

Higginson, Henry L.

    background and character, 85

    BSO's influence on NEC, 29, 51

    death of, 87

    during World War I, 85

    founds Boston Symphony Orchestra, 28

    Jordan Hall inaugural, 13, 14, 69

    philanthropy of, 14, 28, 58

    photo of, 28

    Tourjée, Eben and, 28

    mentioned, 56

Hill, Edward Burlingame, 56, 57, 89

Hindemith, Paul, 87, 120

Hirschfeld, Max, 51

Hoch Conservatory, 49

Hoenich, Richard, 147

Holland, Dave, 134

Holmes

    Malcolm, 106, 108, 113-114, 120, 122

    Oliver Wendell, 43

Holst, Gustav, 79

Holt, H.E., 30

Homer

    Louisa, 77

    Sidney, 77

Honegger, Arthur, 114

honorary degrees, 121, 127, 135

Horticultural Hall, 64, 81

hot dog, introduction of, 56

Houston Symphony Orchestra, 104

Hovey, Alfred, 38, 53

Howe, Julia Ward, 13, 75

Hughes, Richard, 147

Humperdinck, Engelbert, 99

Hyla, Lee, 147

Icor, 103

"If One Generation Can Ever Tell Another" (Friedan), 117

Indian music, 135

Institute for Eurhythmics, 70

Institute of Musical Art (New York), 94

Institute of Technology, 45

International Music Festival, 1955, 119

Iphigenia (Gluck), 78

Isabella Stewart Gardner Museum, 64, 89

Jackson, Raymond, 119

Jadassohn, Salomon, 55

Japan, 29, 30, 105

jazz, 108, 133, 134

Jeanne d'Arc (Converse), 78

Jews in the Soviet Union, 103

Job (Converse), 78

Jochum von Moltke, Veronica, 135, 141

John Philip Sousa Band, 77

John the Baptist (Büchtiger), 114

Joplin, Scott, 136

Jordan

    Eben, 2nd, 91

        background and character, 63, 64

        becomes NEC trustee, 63

        Chadwick, George Whitefield, relationship with, 64

        financial support for NEC, 21, 68, 69, 73

        Jordan Hall inaugural, 13, 14

        new Conservatory building, 64, 65

        philanthropy of, 81, 90

        photo of, 64

        World War I, 83

        mentioned, 15, 119

    Eben, Sr.

        background and character, 63

        financial support for NEC, 35, 40, 63

        Peace Jubilees, 26

        photo of, 26

        Tourjée, Eben, relationship with, 63, 64

        mentioned, 91, 95

    Mrs. Eben (wife of Eben, 2nd)

        Jordan Hall inaugural, 13

    Jordan Hall

        Beethoven statue at, 18, 68

        building and funding, 64, 65, 67-69

        described, 64, 65, 69

        during the Depression, 95, 96

        inauguration of, described, 13, 14, 69

        limitations of, for opera, 114, 115

        National Historic Landmark status, 147

Jordan Hall *(Continued)*

    performances at, 87

        Bernstein, Leonard, 104

        Boatwright, McHenry, 119

        Boulanger, Nadia, 103

        Büchtiger, Fritz, 128

        Busoni, Ferruccio, 77

        centennial concert, 133

        Chadwick, George Whitefield programs, 79

        dePachmann, Vladimir, 77

        during World War I, 86

        during World War II, 106

        Figaro, 128

        first opera, 78

        Goodrich, John Wallace programs, 79

        Hayes, Roland, 118

        Holmes, Malcolm, last by, 114

        Kreisler, Fritz, 77

        Mason, Edith, 77

        Modern Jazz Quartet, 136

        NEC Chorus, 114

        NEC Orchestra under Prausnitz, Frederick, 127

        Norton, Lillian, 77

        Nova Arte Quartet, 127

        opera, 102, 115

        Our Town, 121

        Radamsky, Sergei, 103

        Russian artists, 147

        Tenth Symphony (Shostakovich), 126

        Thibaud, Jacques, 77

        Thompson, Randall, 128

        under Keller, Harrison, 122

    photo of, 54, 59, 66, 71, 72

    restoration of, 118

    sound quality of, 69

    mentioned, 15, 81

Jordan Hall organ, 68, 69

Jordan Marsh department store, 63

Jordan Prize, 79

Juilliard Graduate School, 94, 121, 125

Juilliard School of Music, 140

Kaddish (Bernstein), 128

Kahn, Otto Hermann, 60

Kansas City Philharmonic, 104

Kappa Gamma Psi fraternity, 75

Kaun, Kathleen, 147

Keller, Harrison

    ambitions for NEC, 120, 121

    background, 120

    hires McKay, Ruth, 117

Keller, Harrison (Continued)
   informal style of, 121, 122
   photo of, 121
   rebuilding strategy, 123
   mentioned, 125, 126
Kennedy
   John F., 128
   Joseph P., 33
   Rose Fitzgerald, 33
King
   Coretta Scott, 118, 119, 121, 135
   Martin Luther, Jr., 118
King David (Honegger), 114
Kirchner, Leon, 147
Kirton, Stanley, 119
Klezmer Conservatory Band, 134, 147
Kneisel, Franz, 43, 56
Kogawa no Hotori (Abe), 88
Kohs, Ellis, 108
Korean War, 122
Koussevitzky, Serge, 87, 89, 99, 104, 120
Krasner, Louis, 147
Kreisler, Fritz, 77, 83, 84, 97

La Bohème, 115
Lady Windemere's Fan (Wilde), 36
La Mer (Debussy), 87
Lang, B.J., 24, 50, 56
La Scala, 110
Lehner, Eugene, 147
Leipzig Conservatory, 28
Lesser, Laurence, 135, 136, 144-147
Lévy, Ernst, 108
Lewis, John, 136
Ligeti, György, 147
L'Incoronazione di Poppea (Monteverdi), 115
Lind, Jenny, 20
Little, Alfred, 17
Loeb Theater, 115, 140
Loeffler, Charles Martin, 104
Lombardi, Sarah, 116
London Bach Choir, 79
Longfellow Bridge, 81
Longy, Renée, 70
Lowell Opera Company, 111
Lutoslawski, Witold, 147

Macomber, John, 120
Madama Butterfly, 99
Madame Melba, 44, 52, 83
Madame Parepa-Rosa, 27
Madame Patti, 38, 44

Magic Flute, The, 115
Mahler, Gustav, 126, 133
Mahr, Emil, 38, 44
Making Music Together series, 147
Manahattan School of Music, 140
Manhattan Opera House, 60
Marcuse, Herbert, 121
Marguerita (Chadwick), 55
Mariage aux Lanternes (Offenback), 102
Marienleben (Hindemith), 120
Marine Band, 99
Marriage of Figaro, The, 102
Martino, Donald, 135
Masefield, John, 70
Mason
   Edith, 77
   Lowell, 13, 17, 19, 20, 46, 146
   Luther Whiting, 29, 30, 145
   Stuart, 88
Mason and Hamlin Prize, 95, 104
"Mason-song," 29, 30, 145
Massachusetts Historical Society, 81
Massachusetts Institute of Technology, 140
Massachusetts State House, 46, 47
Mass (Bruckner), 113
Master of Music program, 98
Materna, Amalie, 43
Maurel, Victor, 15
Mayes, Samuel, 127
McKim, Mead, & White, 64, 81
McKinley
   Carl, 104, 113, 121
   William, 75
   William Thomas, 134
Medium (Menotti), 128
Melpomene (Chadwick), 14, 46, 55, 56, 69
Menotti, Gian Carlo, 115, 128
Messiaen, Olivier, 117, 147
Metropolitan Opera Company
   Caldwell, Sarah and, 110
   Curtin, Phyllis at, 110
   during World War I, 84
   Elias, Rosalind, 110
   Homer, Louisa and, 77
   Miller, Mildred at, 115
   Pipe of Desire, The, 78
   radio program, 102
   Steber, Eleanor, 109
   mentioned, 60, 115
Metropolitan Opera Orchestra, 131
Miller
   Gladys, 109, 111

Miller (Continued)
   Mildred, 115
Mills, Frank, 85
minorities at New England Conservatory, 118, 119
Mitropoulos, Dmitri, 123, 125
Modella, La (Bimboni), 61
Modern Jazz Quartet, 136
Moltke, Veronica Jochum von, 135, 141
Monteux, Pierre, 87
Monteverdi, Claudio, 99, 103, 115
Moriarty, John, 122, 147
Moscow Conservatory, 128
Moscow Imperial Opera, 60
Moses, Bob, 134
Moses and Aron (Schoenberg), 114
Mountain Song (Rotoli), 42
movies, music and, 88
Mozart, Wolfgang Amadeus, 107, 133
Mr. Hadley's Ocean (Hadley), 88
Muck, Karl, 78, 84, 85, 87
Munich Conservatory, 28
Mu Phi Epsilon sorority, 75
Museum of Fine Arts (Boston), 15, 21, 89
music. See also American music; specific piece; specific type
   American aversion to serious, 46
   Americanization of orchestral, 88
   during the Depression, 96
   financial state of serious, 140
   impact of World War I, 86
   impulse for identifiably American, 19, 99
   in pre-Civil War America, 19, 20
   movies and, 88
   popular, 98
   technology and, 86, 97
   "third stream," 135, 136
Music Academies, 13
Musical Courier, 57
Musical Herald, The, 30, 38, 47, 63
musical instruments, museum of, 30
musical theory, 70, 124
Musica Sacra, 111
music education in public schools, 19, 20, 31, 146
Music Educators' National Conference, 126
Music Hall
   Beethoven statue, 68
   New England Conservatory leaves, 33
   opera at, 60
   organ, 68
   photo of, 16, 22, 23

Music Hall *(Continued)*

role in the early history of NEC, 22, 24

size of, 40

Tourjée, Eben meets Boston's music leaders at, 17, 18

used while Jordan Hall built, 67

mentioned, 13, 76

"Music in America" (Dvořák), 73

musicology, 127

music therapy, 125

Muxom, Reverend, 38

Mystic Trumpeter (Converse), 97

National Academy of Recording Arts and Sciences, 114

National Conference of Music Educators, 114

National Education Association, 30

National Endowment for the Humanities, 146

National Historic Landmark status, 147

National Institute of Music (Tokyo), 30

National Music Congress (NMC), 29-31

National Music Course (textbook), 30

National Music Teachers' Association, 29, 30, 47, 58

National Peace Jubilee. See Peace Jubilees

National Teachers' Association, 31

Naumburg Award, 111

NBC Radio Network, 91, 97

NEC Big Band, 147

NEC Youth Philharmonic Orchestra, 146

Netsky, Hankus, 134

Neume, The, 74

New Deal, 96, 97

Newell, George, 104

New England Conservatory

alumni in major orchestras, 104

as School of Music, Literature, and Art, 37, 50, 69

band, 98

Boston Symphony Orchestra, 24, 28, 29, 78, 104

Boston University alliance, 29, 50

Brown Hall. See Brown Hall

centennial, 128, 132, 133

chorus, 61, 88, 107, 116. See also New England Conservatory Chorus

Christianity of, 33

Community Services Department, 134, 141

competition with Boston Conservatory of Music, 24, 44, 51

concert for peace, 1970, 137

New England Conservatory *(Continued)*

contemporary music, 103, 104, 133

degree granting authority, 89

Department of Music for Young People, 121

during the Depression, 93-98

during Vietnam War, 136, 137

during World War I, 83, 85-87

during World War II, 102, 106

endowment. See endowment

enrollment. See enrollment

European luminaries at, in the late 1880s, 38-40

faculty animosity with Faelten, Carl, 51-53

finances

after World War II, 108

at the death of Tourjée, Eben, 49

crisis of 1970-71, 140

under Aliferis, James, 126

under Allen, Philip, 113, 120

under Chadwick, George Whitefield, 73, 93

under Faelten, Carl, 51, 52

under Falender, Andrew, 143

under Goodrich, John Wallace, 94-97

under Keller, Harrison, 122, 123

under Schuller, Gunther, 131, 132, 135, 140-143

under Tourjée, Eben, 37, 40, 45, 46

under Williams, Chester, 126, 128, 129

first commencement, 29

graduate programs

doctor of musical arts, 123, 124, 146

Master's program added, 98

graduation rates, 37, 44, 46, 117

growth after World War II, 107

inaugural concert, 19

incorporated, 38

initial proposal for and rejection of, 17, 18

international students at, 116, 117, 145

jazz, 133, 134

Jordan Hall. See Jordan Hall

kind of students attracted to, 24, 33, 99, 113, 117

merger talks, 140

museum of musical instruments, 30

National Historic Landmark status, 147

opera at. See opera

orchestra, 132. See also New England Conservatory Orchestra

photo of, 129

physical plant, 124

New England Conservatory *(Continued)*

popular music, 98, 99, 113, 125

prestige and stature, 95, 116, 123, 140

recast as college of music, 120

recording studio, 97

reshaped by Schuller, Gunther, 131, 132

scholarships. See scholarships

Sleeper Hall. See Sleeper Hall

St. James Hotel. See St. James Hotel

star system, 38-40, 50

"third stream" music, 135, 136

ties with Russian musicians, 126, 128

tuning program, 49, 69

unified campus, 145

weekly broadcasts begun, 97

New England Conservatory Chorus

Brooks, Tamara, 147

tours Europe, 142

under Cooke deVaron, Lorna, 114

New England Conservatory Magazine, 67, 84, 85

New England Conservatory Orchestra

at Jordan Hall, 78

Burgin, Richard and, 120

Carnegie Hall, 146, 147

Chadwick, George Whitefield starts, 59, 60

champions American music, 88

changes under Koussevitzky, Serge, 87

distinguishes itself, 88

during World War I, 84

during World War II, 106

first attempts to form, 44, 45, 52

Goodrich, Wallace and, 93

growth after World War II, 107, 108, 113

Hoenich, Richard and, 147

importance of, 116, 147

leads Americanization of other orchestras, 88

Musican Courier ridicules, 57

musicianship of, 88, 89

photo of, 88

Prausnitz, Frederick conducts, 127

radio performances, 97

repertoire, 88, 108

tours Europe, 142

under Schuller, Gunther, 133

New England Conservatory Ragtime Ensemble, 136, 138, 139

New England Normal Institute, 30

New England Opera Theater, 102, 110, 115

New England Triptych (Schuman), 127

"New Generation" program, 135

Newport Musical Institute, 20

New York City Opera, 111

New York Philharmonic Orchestra, 128

Nickrenz, Scott, 135, 147

Night Music (Rochberg), 127

Ninth Symphony (Beethoven), 114

Nordica. See Norton, Lillian

Nordquist, Irvin, 108

Normal Musical Institute, 29

Northeastern College, 89

Northeastern University, 115, 123, 140, 145

North End Mission, 47

Norton, Lillian (Nordica)

 background and character, 76

 describes studying at NEC, 24

 photo of, 25

 recalls concerts in the Music Hall, 22

 success aided NEC, 24

 Tourjée, Eben and, 36

 women's rights, 76, 77

 mentioned, 44, 46, 109

Notre Dame Academy, 89

Nova Arte Quartet, 127

Oberlin Conservatory, 20, 119

O'Brien, Hugh, 33, 42

Octet (Stravinsky), 120

Ode (Chadwick), 56

Oedipus Tyrannus (Paine), 47

Offenback, Jacques, 102, 136

Old Maid and the Thief (Menotti), 115

Olivet College, 55

O'Neill, John, 24, 76

opera

 after Goldovsky, Boris, 128

 Bimboni, Oreste starts, program, 60, 61

 during World War II, 102

 Faelten, Carl promotes, study, 51

 Gilbert, Clayton directs, 61

 Goodrich, John Wallace brings back, 99

 importance of, 116

 in Boston, 60

 money problems close, program, 128

 NEC's first full opera, 61, 78

 program returned in 1989, 146, 147

 program returns, 146, 147

 study of, fades, 114

 under Goldovsky, Boris, 102, 109, 115

Opera Company of Boston (earlier called

 Opera Group of Boston), 110, 111

Opera Magazine, 83

"Opera on the Air" (radio program), 102, 109

orchestra. See New England Conservatory

 Orchestra

Orfeo (Monteverdi), 99

Overture in Bohemia (Hadley), 88

Owen, Wilfred, 86

Pachmann, Vladimir de, 77

Paderewski, Ignacy

 during World War I, 83, 84

 performs at Sleeper Hall, 43, 52

 photo of, 43

 mentioned, 22, 77, 97

Paderewski Prize, 79

Padrone, The (Chadwick), 79

Paine, John Knowles, 13, 19, 47, 56, 113

Pan-Hellenic Society, 75

Paradise and the Peri (Schumann), 113

Parepa-Rosa, Madame, 27

Paris Conservatorie, 116

Paris Opera, 111

Parker, Horatio, 88

Pastoral Symphony (Williams), 88

Patterson, Mary, 53

Pattison, Lee, 96

Peabody Award, 109

Peabody Institute (Baltimore), 20, 49

Peace Jubilees

 impact of, 27, 31

 launching and description of, 26, 27, 29

 publicity for, aids NEC, 24

 mentioned, 55, 63, 141

Pell, Claiborne, 121

Pelléas et Mélisande, 140

Pergolesi, Giovanni Battista, 99

Perin, George, 64

Perkins, Charles, 18, 68

Perlman, Itzhak, 128

Pershing, John Joseph, 86, 120

Petrograd Conservatory, 120

Philharmonic Society, 55, 58

Phillips

 Harvey, 125, 132

 Thomas, 128

Phi Mu Alpha Sinfonia, 75

Piano Concerto (Bartók), 87

piano department, 52, 53

Piatigorsky, Gregor, 144, 147

Pierrot Lunaire (Schoenberg), 120

Pi Kappa Lambda, 117

Pinkham, Daniel, 114, 127, 128

Pipe of Desire, The (Converse), 78

Piston, Walter, 57, 103, 113, 126, 128

Pittsburgh Orchestra, 77

Polish Victims' Relief Fund, 83

popular music, 98, 99, 125

Porgy and Bess (Gershwin), 120

Porter, Quincy

 changing student body, 117

 contemporary music and, 103, 108

 opera, 102

 photo of, 104

 resigns, 119

 takes over, 104

 World War II, 106

 mentioned, 121

Prausnitz, Frederick, 127

Presser, Theodore, 29

Price, Leontyne, 125

prison program, 134

Proctor, Leland, 113

Prokofiev, Sergey, 108

Providence Conservatory of Music, 20

Providence Institute of Music, 20

Providence (R.I.) Journal, 84, 85

Prudential Center concerts, 141

Psalm of Thanksgiving (Mahler), 133

Psalm XCVIII, A Sacred Cantata (Schuller),

 133

Psyché (Franck), 78, 104

Puccini, Giacomo, 99, 115, 128

Pulitzer Prize, 135

Puritan Passions (movie), 88

Quartet for the End of Time (Messiaen), 117

Quartet No. 3 (Chadwick), 56

Quartet No. 5 (Chadwick), 56

Quintet for Pianoforte and Strings, 113

Rachmaninoff, Sergey, 97, 104

Radamsky, Sergei, 103

Radaud, Henri, 87

Radcliffe College, 89, 114

Radcliffe Glee Club, 77

radio, influence on music, 86

Radio City, 99

Raff, Joachim, 38, 49

Ragtime Ensemble, 136, 138, 139

Railroad Galop, 20

Rainbow Room, 99

Ramanathan, Professor, 132

Ravel, Maurice, 86, 114, 133

Red Cross, 86

Reio Bravo (Newell), 104

Requiem (Berlioz), 114

Rhapsody on a Persian Air (Mason), 88

Rheinberger, Josef
  Chadwick, George Whitefield and, 75, 79
  classicism of, 86
  Concerto in F, 60
  students who studied with, 55, 70, 77
  work banned during World War I, 84
  mentioned, 93, 103
Riders to the Sea (Vaughan Williams), 110
Rip Van Winkle (Chadwick), 55
Robinson, Governor, 42, 45
Rockefeller, Mrs. John D., 123, 129, 141
Rockefeller Foundation, 123, 141
Rogers, Clara Kathleen, 94, 113
Romanza Andaluza (Sarasate), 42
Roosevelt
  Franklin D., 96
  Teddy, 63
Rosalie, the Prairie Flower, 58
Rosenbaum, Victor, 144
Rosenblith, Eric, 135
Rotoli, Augusto, 38, 42
Rounds for Stings (Diamon), 108
Row, Peter, 135, 136
Rubinstein
  Anton, 42
  Arthur, 15, 77
Rubinstein Competition, 50
Russell, George, 133, 134

Sabine, Wallace C., 69
Sacrifice (Converse), 78
Saint of Bleecker Street (Menotti), 128
Saint-Saëns, Camille, 79, 104
Sanromá, Jesús, 86, 126
Santlemann, William, 99
Sarasate, Pablo de, 42
Sauret, Emile, 52
Sayre, Jesse Wilson, 86
Schlemiel, 147
Schoenberg, Arnold Franz Walter, 86, 87, 103, 114, 120, 143
scholarships
  Chadwick, George Whitefield seeks money for, 73, 75
  during the Depression, 94, 95
  Gladys Childs Miller, 111
  more sought, 123
  new, 113
  opera, 102
  popular music, 102
School of Music (at East Greenwich Academy), 20

schools of music. See conservatories and schools of music
Schuller, Gunther
  background and character, 131
  community services, 135
  during the Vietnam War, 136
  musical tastes of, 133, 136
  named president of NEC, 131
  photo of, 133
  resigns, 142, 143
  tours Europe with NEC Orchestra, 142
  vision for and reshaping of NEC, 131, 132, 134, 135
  mentioned, 144, 146
Schuman, William, 127
Schumann
  Clara, 38, 49
  Robert, 113, 114
Schweitzer, Albert, 116, 117
Scudder, David, 141
SDS, 136, 137
Second Etude (Rubinstein), 42
Second Hurricane (Copland), 104
Second Symphony (Hartmann), 127
Serkin, Peter, 128
Serva Padrona (Pergolesi), 99
Session, Roger, 127
Seven Studies on Themes by Paul Klee (Schuller), 135
Shawmut Congregational Church, 67
Shepherd, Arthur, 56, 70, 89, 113
  Aliferis, James as student of, 123
  background, 79
  during World War I, 86
  Works Progress Administration, 96
Sherman
  Cecile, 99
  Russell, 135
Shostakovich, Dmitri, 108, 126
Sigma Alpha Iota sorority, 75, 76
Sills, Beverly, 110, 121
Silverstein, Joseph, 127
Simmons College, 77, 89, 127
Sinfonia Club, 74, 75
Sixth Symphony (Mennin), 127
Sleeper, Jacob, 40
Sleeper Hall
  described, 42
  drawing of, 41-43
  Faelten, Carl, last performance of, 53
  financing of, 40
  importance of, 43, 44

Sleeper Hall *(Continued)*
  limitations of, 45, 59
  performances at, 43, 49, 52, 77
  used while Jordan Hall built, 67
  mentioned, 61
Smetana, Bedrich, 115
Smith, Warren Storye, 122
Smith Alumnae Quarterly, 117
solfeggio, 50, 52, 70, 107
Sonata No. 2 (Grieg), 42
Sonatina for Pianoforte, 113
sororities, 75. See also specific organization
Sosarme (Handel), 42
Soviet Union, 103, 147
Spanish-American War, 59, 75
Spaulding (Harriet) Charitable Trust, 123
St. Botolph building, 145
St. James Hotel
  cost of, 40, 45
  drawing of, 32, 40, 41
  limits of, 61
  NEC at, 33, 35, 36
  NEC leaves, 64
  photo of, 35
  mentioned, 26
Steber, Eleanor, 102, 109, 115, 121, 125
Sterling, Hattie, 19
Stern, Issac, 127
Stickney, Virginia, 77
Still, William Grant, 118, 119
Stokowski, Leopold, 77
Strauss, Richard, 84, 115
Stravinsky, Igor Fyodorovich, 86, 87, 103, 120
Students for a Democratic Society (SDS), 136, 137
Suite Symphonic (Chadwick), 79
Suor Angelica (Puccini), 99
Susannah (Floyd), 115, 126
Swing, 99
Symphony Hall, 13, 15, 64, 69, 71, 81
Symphony in D (Converse), 70
Symphony in D (Haydn), 60
Szumowska-Adamowski, Antoinette, 13, 44, 70, 83, 84

Tam O'Shanter (Chadwick), 79
Tanglewood, 104, 110
Tasogare (Abe), 88
Tchaikovsky, Piotr Ilyitch, 102
Tenth Symphony (Shostakovich), 126
Thelonious Monk Institute of Jazz Performance, 146

Thibaud, Jacques, 77

"third stream" music, 135, 136

Third Symphony (Bruckner), 127

Third Symphony (Chadwick), 56

Third Symphony (Mahler), 126

Thomas, Theodore, 13, 20, 22, 56

Thompson

    Marcus, 147

    Randall, 114, 128, 133

Time Magazine, 110

Tippett, Michael, Sir, 147

Tobey, Miss, 46

Toho Music School, 147

Tokyo Conservatory of Music, 30

Tourjée

    Abbie (wife of Eben), 22

    Eben

        African American students, 118, 134

        ambitions for an orchestra, 44, 45, 59

        at NEC 1870 to 1880, 29

        background and character, 17, 20, 21,

            29, 31, 35, 36

        dies, 49

        enrollment under, 52

        establishes tie to Japan, 30

        hires Faelten, Carl, 49

        his health fails, 45, 47

        historical context of, 58

        incorporates the conservatory, 38

        Jordan, Eben, Sr., and, 63, 64

        launches New England Conservatory,

            18

        length of service, 119

        meets Boston's music leaders, 17

        Musical Herald, The, 38

        Music Hall organ, 68

        Norton, Lillian and, 24

        organizations founded by, 20, 22, 29

        Peace Jubilees, 26, 27, 31

        philosophy of, 21, 22, 29, 36, 37, 45-47

        photo of, 17, 31, 49

        promotion efforts of, 24, 29, 35

        proposes conservatory, 17, 18

        star system of, 38

        women at NEC, 33, 35, 36

        mentioned, 13, 15, 50, 51, 53, 55, 64,

            116, 129, 144-146

Tourjée Memorial Student Aid Fund, 75

Transformation (Schuller), 135

Tremont Temple, 60, 67

Tufts University, 57, 94

tuning department, 48, 69

Turn of the Screw (Britten), 115

24th Massachusetts Volunteers, 26

Une Voix dans le Desert (Cammaerts), 86

United States Marine Band, 99

Upham, J. Baxter, 17, 18, 20, 22

U.S. Information Service, 119

U.S. Office of Education, 31

U.S. Park Service, 147

U.S. State Department, 116

U.S. War Department, 86

Ushioda, Masuko, 135

Vallecillo, Irma, 147

Van Ness, Nellie, 76

Vaughan Williams, Ralph, 79, 88, 102, 108,

    110, 114

Verrot, Pascal, 147

Vienna Imperial Opera House, 60

Vienna Staatsoper, 110, 111

Vietnam War, 135, 136, 140

Viking's Last Voyage (Chadwick), 55

Violin Concerto (Dukelsky), 120

Violin Sonata (Shepherd), 70

Visitation (Schuller), 131, 135

Vitous, Miroslav, 134

"*Voice of Firestone, The*" radio program, 125

Vox Humana, 38

Wagner

    Cosima, 22, 76

    Richard, 60, 84

Walnut Hill School, 146

WBJ, 91, 97

WBZ, 97

Webern, Anton, 86, 87, 103

Weston, Randy, 134

WGBH, 127, 146

WHDH, 97

Wheelwright, Edmund, 64, 65, 69, 81

Wheelwright and Haven, 64, 81

When Johnny Comes Marching Home

    (Gilmore), 26

whirl...ds (I) (Cogan), 133

Whiting

    Albert, 94

    George, 55

    Wiant, Bliss, 105

Wilde, Oscar, 36

Williams, Chester

Williams, Chester *(Continued)*

    as dean, 123

    as young teacher, 107

    changes initiated, 128

    named president, 126

    NEC finances, 129

    photo of, 127

    recalls Miller, Gladys, 111

    resigns, 129

    Schuller, Gunther and, 132, 133

    vision for New England Conservatory, 127

Wilson

    Gerald, 134

    Phil, 134

    Woodrow, 84, 86

women

    as students at NEC, 33, 35, 36, 44, 75, 76,

        117

    opportunities for, in music, 44, 77, 105

    political views on education for, 46, 47

    "redundant," 36, 46

    role in growth of the arts, 19

    social constraints on, in the 1980s, 35, 36

Women's Christian Temperance Union, 46

Women's Orchestra of Los Angeles, 77

Women's Social and Political Union, 76

women's suffrage, 36, 42, 75, 76

Women's Symphony Orchestra, 104, 105

Works Progress Administration (WPA), 96, 97

World Peace Jubilee. See Peace Jubilees

World's Columbian Exposition, 55

World War I

    impact on NEC, 83, 85-87

    intolerance during, 84, 85

    mentioned, 88

World War II, 96, 102, 105-107

Yale University, 57, 88, 119

Yenching College, 116

Yiddish music, 134

Young Ladies' Missionary Society, 36

Young Men's Christian Association (YMCA),

    29, 36, 47, 63, 89, 90

Young Women's Christian Association

    (YWCA), 86

Youth Philharmonic Orchestra, 146

Zander

    Benjamin, 135, 146

    Patricia, 135

Zerrahn, Carl, 18, 26, 27, 50

"Appalachian Spring"

Alice Tully

Maxwell Davies

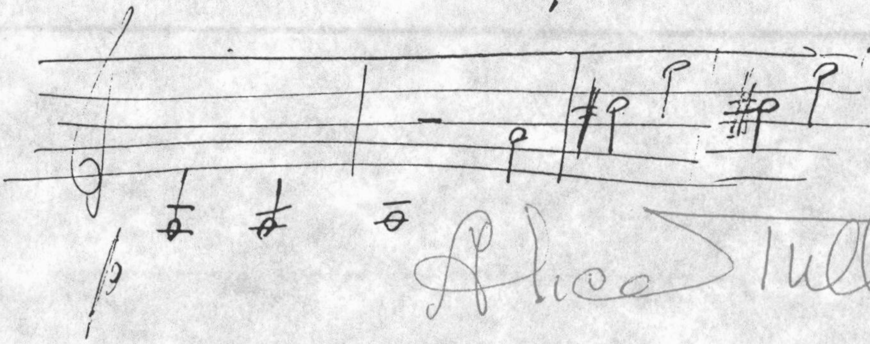

With all best wishes to the

NEW ENGLAND Conservatory of Music

and its director Harrison Keller

Aaron Copland

Boston Nov 30, 1950

Marian

pour Laurence Lesser,
en souvenir du concert de mes oeuvres
au Conservatoire "New England" de Boston,
et des quatre concerts où Seiji Ozawa a
dirigé "Saint François d'Assise" également à Boston.
Merci pour tout!

Olivier Messiaen

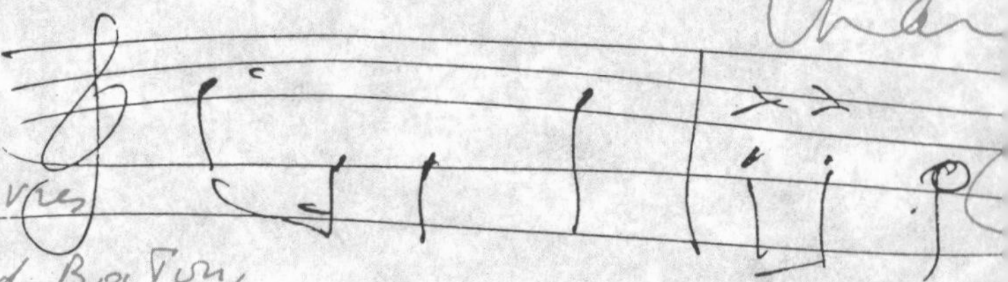

Gunther A. Schuller

All the best in life

Jan Peerce

To the New England Conservatory family,
You are the embodiment of a living tradition. It is truly an honor to be affiliated with this institution; as a parent and recipient of a honorary degree.
With greatest

It is a great honour for me to receive an honorary Degree in the famous New England Conservatory of Music

Witold Lutosławski

October 29th, 1990

Coretta